"Lew Sterrett's *Life Lessons from a Horse Whisperer* is as captivating as one of his live Sermon on the Mount presentations. Fascinating horse experiences, shedding insights that help us better understand their master's Master!"
- **Dan T. Cathy**, *President & COO, Chick-fil-A, Inc.*

"Profoundly engaging! You'll be captivated by the real-life experiences of this world-class horse whisperer – and then be stopped in your tracks by the applied truths he offers. Must reading for excitement and life-giving insights."
- **Bob Kobielush**, *President, Christian Camp and Conference Association*

"Lew Sterrett has spent a lifetime learning what it takes to capture the heart of a horse, and in the process how to communicate invaluable life lessons for people. I thoroughly enjoyed *Life Lessons from a Horse Whisperer*."
- *Jane Austin Graham*, *wife of Franklin Graham, President and CEO of Samaritan's Purse and the Billy Graham Evangelistic Association*

"Lew Sterrett is a communicator who cares for and connects with his readers as he cares
He is a horse whisperer wl
- *Todd J. Williams, Ph.D.,*
University

D1055766

"Lew's book helped us to understand this amazing man as well as his ministry on a deeper level. His ability to use examples of horses and life made it easy to understand and enjoyable to read."
- **Stacy Westfall**, *professional horse trainer and first woman to win the Road to the Horse competition*

"Hard work and trust. These are Lew Sterrett's prescription for successful relationships – for humans and horses. I agree!"
- **Les Steckel**, *President/CEO of the Fellowship of Christian Athletes*

Dr Lew Sterrett is Executive Director of the Miracle Mountain Ranch near Erie, Pennsylvania. He is a licensed pastor and a certified youth, marriage and family counselor through the United Association of Christian Counselors. www.sermononthemount.org

Bob Smietana is an award-winning religion writer and contributing editor for *Christianity Today* magazine. He is currently religion writer for *The Tennessean* in Nashville.

LIFE LESSONS
FROM A
HORSE WHISPERER

Dr. Lew Sterrett
with Bob Smietana

MONARCH
BOOKS

Oxford, UK & Grand Rapids, Michigan, USA

Represented by: Janet Kobobel Grant, Books and Such Literary Agency, 4788 Carissa Ave., Santa Rosa, CA 95405, Tel: 707-538-4184
Email: janet@booksandsuch.biz

First published in the UK in 2010 by Monarch Books
(a publishing imprint of Lion Hudson plc),
Wilkinson House, Jordan Hill Road, Oxford OX2 8DR.
Tel: +44 (0)1865 302750 Fax: +44 (0)1865 302757
Email: monarch@lionhudson.com
www.lionhudson.com

ISBN: 978-1-85424-918-0 (UK)
ISBN: 978-0-8254-6316-7 (USA)

Distributed by:
UK: Marston Book Services Ltd, PO Box 269, Abingdon, Oxon OX14 4YN;
USA: Kregel Publications, PO Box 2607, Grand Rapids, Michigan 49501

Unless otherwise stated, Scripture quotations are taken from the Holy Bible, New International Version, © 1973, 1978, 1984 by the International Bible Society. Used by permission of Hodder & Stoughton Ltd. All rights reserved.

This book has been printed on paper and board independently certified as having come from sustainable forests.

British Library Cataloguing Data
A catalogue record for this book is available from the British Library.

Printed and bound in the United States of America.

CONTENTS

Dedication to the Team

My wife, family (immediate and extended), staff, friends, volunteers, and supporters are the real people who make this book happen. No one ever truly succeeds or suffers alone.

Acknowledgments

To my wife, Dr. Melodie Sterrett, whose sacrifice is immeasurable. Despite demanding schedules, ceaseless travel, and overwhelming pressure, her inspiration and faithfulness is the substance of much of what I live and present.

Bob Smietana proved to be a gift from God. His down-to-earth, easy manner and diligent efforts brought this book into being. He helped me translate horse terminology for the average reader.

Literary agent Janet Kobobel Grant and Editorial Director Tony Collins of Lion Hudson provided the professional experience and confidence to get this story told.

Thanks also to a host of photographers. Charlie Hilton is a photographer above par, and a man of generous spirit. Donnie Rosie was not only resourceful with photos, but believed in this project before I did. Thanks. Photos were also supplied by Caleb Martin, Hannah O'Brien, Summer Poche, and Laura Clawson.

I also owe a deep debt of gratitude to those who have provided horses for this ministry. Warren and Mary Davis continued in the vein of her parents, J.W. and Betty Bailey, of providing quality stock for the ministry. Berry, Spark, and Romeo are among them. Spotlite is from the home of Benham and Louise Stewart, owners of Singing Pines Plantation and breeders of world-champion horses. Thousands of other horses were provided through our Sermon on the Mount hosts throughout the years.

May the men and women who traveled with Sermon on the Mount over the years as my assistants receive an eternal reward for their investment.

Through the years, Ward Studebaker had the most significant impact on my horse training values, starting with my university experience. Countless contributors, including Doug Milholland, John Lyons, and Kathleen Kronk, have had an encouraging influence.

I am grateful for associates who took time out of their busy schedules to read and add their endorsement to this book: Dan T. Cathy, Jane Graham, Bob Kobielush, Les Steckel, Jesse and Stacy Westfall, and Dr. Todd Williams.

There are countless others whose behind-the-scenes sacrifices are noteworthy, but let it be said on behalf of them and of myself that all credit really belongs to God. For apart from a relationship with God through Jesus Christ, we can do nothing.

FOREWORD

This is more than a book about horses, as one might suppose. It is a story about life and hope: hope that prevails in the unknown, hope that prevails in adversity, and hope that prevails even through death itself.

It provokes the question of how hope can prevail and on what basis. Is it possible to have hope, even joy, amidst great trials in life? The essence of this story is to look at some of life's perplexing circumstances through the eyes of a horse. One can only imagine the feelings a horse might have when he is corralled, roped, saddled, harnessed, and ridden or driven for the first time.

In each of our lives, there are circumstances, people, and situations that can and do provoke all of us to fear, dismay, and even rebellion like a horse. It is my hope that you will gain a fresh perspective and be empowered to respond more effectively and successfully to those things which tend to steal away your hope.

As a counselor, I never expect anyone to really make any substantial change unless they can find a sound and trustworthy basis for renewed hope. This also is true in the life of a horse. Yet, like his peers, he is prone to believe that hope comes from escaping the rider, the bridle, or the fence.

The hope of a true and lasting reward is essential in capturing motivation. When we understand these essentials, we discover the keys to confidence, power, and seamless oneness. I trust that the life lessons of this story will result in a new and lasting hope for you.

CHAPTER 1

DO YOU TRUST ME?

I T STARTED OUT as an ordinary trail ride.

In April 2003, I set out with Spotlight, a young Quarter Horse stallion I'd been training, to get some exercise. He'd been in a trailer most of the previous day, as we were on our way from our ranch in Spring Creek, Pennsylvania to Kansas City, Missouri, to take part in an Equus America event, run by the trainer John Lyons. Along the way, we stopped to visit a friend, who'd invited me to speak at a gathering she had organized.

Spotlight was about four at the time, but had only been in training a few months. He's an unusual case. He grew up at the Singing Pines Plantation in Glenwood, Georgia, and I'd first seen him not long after he was born. His parents were both dynamic horses, and much was expected of this young colt. On the day of his birth, Spotlight looked perfect. He had a golden coat, a white mane and tail, and seemed strong and healthy.

But there was one problem. On his side was a large white spot—as if someone had turned a spotlight on him. That discoloration made him, in essence, worthless. The spot disqualified him from being registered as a Quarter Horse, and while he could be registered as a Paint Horse, he would be an unlikely Paint Stallion, because of his Quarter Horse bloodlines.

So for his first three years, Spotlight was left on his own. He was well fed and cared for, but had no training. He wasn't trained to lead or to ride, or shown how to do many of the useful tasks horses can accomplish. He had an even-tempered personality and was well loved, but no one knew exactly what to do with him.

His owners, who were friends of ours, offered to lend Spotlight to me for a Sermon on the Mount program, where I rode him for the first time. They eventually gave him to me, and so he ended up coming to live at our ranch. My other horse, Top Cat, was getting older, and so I decided to train Spotlight to take his place one day. We'd been working together for a few months when I thought he was ready to go out on the road.

After a long day of driving, we finally pulled into my friends' Missouri ranch, and got the horses and crew settled down for the night. The next morning, I took Spotlight out for a ride. My friends live at a ranch nestled on a mountainside, and so we enjoyed taking in the scenery. My thought was to ride for several miles, and then come back and get ready for the presentation.

About halfway through the ride, we left the road and walked across a pasture to a small pond. As we went along, the ground started getting muddy due to heavy rainfall the night before, and I realized if we went much farther, we'd start tearing up the lawn. So we took a shortcut, heading through some woods and making our way back to the road. Already my thoughts were turning to the details of the presentation I was to lead.

The retreat was a gathering of homeschoolers, and I wondered, with the heavy rains, if enough people were going to show up to make it worth the effort. I also knew we had to get back on the road not long after the presentation to get to Kansas City on time.

Just then, Spotlight came to a stop. He'd not done that before, and I thought he'd gotten distracted or lost track of what he was supposed to be doing. So I told him to move— we were on a tight schedule and didn't have time for him to fool around. But he would not move.

There were times, earlier in my horse-training experience, when I might have assumed that Spotlight was being obstinate, and pushed him to obey, just as a boss or parent might do. Many of us have that reaction, when someone seems to resist our authority. Still, I knew that Spotlight was a good horse, trustworthy and hardworking, always eager to please. I decided to take time to listen to him first. When I looked down, my heart nearly stopped.

There, across his forearm, was a strand of barbed wire. We had run into a fallen-down barbed-wire fence, which can prove disastrous for a horse. When a horse gets caught up in barbed wire, he doesn't think, he only reacts. The result is catastrophic, if not fatal, with the horse suffering lacerations down to the bone. Even if the horse recovers, he is often scarred for life. Barbed-wire wounds are also prone to infection, and the healing process is long and tedious.

I thought we were fortunate that Spotlight had halted in time to avoid being entangled in the fence. So I picked up the reins and turned to go right, but he would not move. That was not a good sign. Stepping off of Spotlight, I took a closer look. Both his rear legs were also caught in barbed wire. The wire, hidden by underbrush, had encircled his legs in a figure eight. In the middle of a quiet, ordinary trail ride, Spotlight had become trapped. One false move, and he—and I—could face a gruesome death.

If you know anything about horses, you know that when a horse is trapped, he panics. He goes ballistic and does not quit. He does not stop and think, he just reacts and tries to run as fast as he can. It's a survival instinct that keeps him alive in the wild.

But wrapped up in barbed wire, panicking was the absolute worst thing Spotlight could do. Any movement would draw the barbed wire even tighter around his legs, causing him to panic more. I could see it all unfolding in my mind's eye. If Spotlight bolted now, he wouldn't quit. He would wrap both of us in barbed wire and we could both die. The more he struggled, the tighter the wire would wrap around him, and with each desperate movement, his flesh would be torn from his body.

If I tried to free Spotlight, he could kill me as well. The chances were high that I'd get caught in the wire and Spotlight would kick and tear me to death as well.

For the first time in years, I was absolutely terrified. I had no wire-cutters to free Spotlight. I had no cell phone to call for help. There seemed no way out. I've seen horses panic and beat themselves to death against the side of a trailer, or kill themselves by getting tangled up in a fence. I once saw a horse panic and throw herself to the ground so hard that it killed her. The wise thing to do, as cruel as it sounds, would have been to turn and walk away and at least save myself.

But I didn't have the heart to leave Spotlight. To stay was stupid. To leave was terrible and heartless. I felt ashamed and angry. Here I was, a trainer with decades of experience, and I was helpless to save this horse who had put his trust in me. Seeing no solution, I cried out, "Oh God, help me."

Chances are you've uttered that prayer at least once in your life. Maybe it was in a doctor's office, where you or someone you loved first heard the word "cancer." Or perhaps it was a phone call in the middle of the day, saying your child was in the principal's office, or at the police station, or had been in a car wreck. It could have been the time when you were summoned to the boss's office and told that your services were no longer required, or when a foreclosure notice came from the bank. Maybe your spouse said she didn't love you anymore. And you knew that one false move, one wrong word spoken in anger, could ruin everything.

Most of the crises in our lives come like that, out of the blue. "The real troubles in your life," Mary Schmich, a columnist from the *Chicago Tribune* once wrote, "are apt to be things that never crossed your worried mind; the kind that blindside you at 4 p.m. on some idle Tuesday." We worry all the time, and still we never see life-shattering events coming.

We live in a world full of pitfalls and crises. And how we react to them will determine the course of our lives. Just like Spotlight, the smallest thing, one wrong step, can ruin us.

In the moment of my prayer for help with Spotlight, a thought popped into my mind. A week earlier, another trainer had shown me a technique for getting a horse to raise its feet. If I tried to reach back and grab Spotlight's rear leg, I'd throw him off balance, and that would pull the wire tighter and spook him. But if I could reach back and squeeze his hock—which is a joint higher up on the rear leg—Spotlight would lift his foot, and step out of danger.

After taking a deep breath and whispering another

prayer, I reached back and squeezed Spotlight's hock. He lifted his rear foot, and slipped it out of the snare, causing the tension on the barbed wire to ease a bit.

One leg down, three more to go. Another breath and another prayer, and I reached back and squeezed the other hock. Rather than kick and fight, Spotlight lifted his leg right out of the snare, and set it down beside the wire.

We were halfway there. Still, the danger remained. If he bolted now, with both front legs still entangled, Spotlight's skin would be torn to the bone. But in our previous training, I'd taught Spotlight another trick. I would tie a rope around his front feet and teach him not to react or try to free his feet. Instead of resisting when I pulled on the rope, Spotlight learned to yield and follow.

So I put my hand around his left front foot and lifted it up—and rather then resist, Spotlight trusted me, and allowed me to gently pull him out of danger. The right foot soon followed, and he was free. I stepped over the barbed wire, which now lay loose on the ground, and led Spotlight safely back to the road.

I'd like to take credit for saving Spotlight's life; to say that the reason he made it free of the barbed wire without a scratch was because I'm a miracle-working, horse-whispering genius. But that wouldn't be the truth. The real hero in this story is

Spotlight, who overcame his fear, and put his faith and trust in me. His courage and faith in that moment of crisis made all the difference.

Trust remains the building block of every human relationship: between parents and children; between workers and their boss; between a husband and a wife; between people and God. Most of us know this. But it's one thing to know that trust is important, and it's another to take active steps, day by day, to build that trust.

I learned that lesson the hard way, from a horse named Nava Rose.

I first met Nava Rose when I was twenty and working for a local horse breeder. At that time, I thought I was hot stuff. After beginning 4-H when I was eight years old, I'd won three national titles and had a room packed with trophies. More than anything, I loved the praise that came with winning. My horses, when they did what I told them, made me look good and earned me the praise of veteran trainers. That was important to me.

My Dad died when I was five, and though my Mom later remarried, his absence loomed large over my life. I grew up thinking that I didn't matter much and was constantly looking for someone to fill the void in my life. So the older horse trainers and leaders became surrogate father figures. Pleasing them took away some of the pain and grief I felt from missing Dad. My very identity and self-worth were on the line every time I worked with a horse. And failure was not an option.

One summer, my boss entrusted me with Nava Rose, a three-year-old mare with the potential to be a national champion show horse. She'd already mastered the basics, and it was my job to push her to learn more complex tasks. I took her out to the back 40, and started work on a particularly difficult maneuver. I placed a tire on the ground and asked her to place her front feet in the center of it. Then I climbed in the saddle and asked her to turn in a circle, while keeping both front legs in the tire and rotating her back legs.

The longer we worked, the more it became clear that Nava Rose just wasn't getting it.

She'd start circling and then panic and lose her focus. First she started stepping forward out of the tire, ruining the maneuver. Once I cured her of that, she started backing up instead.

I'd not had a lot of experience with failure up to that point, and Nava Rose's struggle with the tire started my anger boiling. A smarter or more experienced trainer would have taken a break or tried a different approach. But I was a young horse-training prodigy, and no stubborn three-year-old mare would spoil my reputation.

So I pushed her harder. All I was asking her to do was keep her front legs in the tire. How hard could that be? So I yelled, kicked, and jerked on her. After all, that's what I'd seen other trainers do. They saw training as a test of will and would do whatever it took to conquer a horse and force it to obey.

But despite my yelling and insistence that Nava Rose do things my way, she didn't get it. Finally, I lost it. She started circling and then got her feet caught up in the tire and backed up. I was so frustrated and angry that I stepped off of her and grabbed her by her head and threw her on the ground.

I was a little shocked because she weighed 1,000 pounds, and horses don't throw down easily. Nava Rose lay on the ground, bewildered and shaking. I sat down on the tire and wept. I have just ruined everything I have invested in her, I thought.

Thankfully, Nava Rose was stunned but not injured. She got up right away, and after a few minutes I went over to her and apologized. I hugged her and told her I was sorry; I had no idea if she understood any of that. Then I told God that I was an idiot—that I was impatient and angry and had acted like a fool.

That day was a breakthrough for me. Nava Rose didn't have a problem. I had a problem. I'd asked her to do too much, too fast, and punished her when she couldn't keep up. That's a problem many of us face—when someone won't do what we say, we try to force them to comply. Nava Rose made me look bad, and I couldn't handle it.

At our ranch we think of horses in two categories: "want to" and "have to." The "have to" horses are perfectly good workers. They are safe to ride and do what they are told, most of the time. But the "want to" horses are the ones who excel. What we try to do in training—for both horses and the young guests who come and stay with us—is to capture their "want to." Every trainer is looking for a "want to" horse, just like every parent wants a child who is eager to listen and learn.

Nava Rose helped me learn how to capture the "want to." I had to re-earn her trust and rebuild her confidence. She was afraid to fail because she knew that if she failed, I would punish her. So I stopped trying to lead by fear and intimidation, and looked for ways to build her confidence.

We reached this goal by making the task bite-sized. First, I stood beside her as we walked through the process. I had her place her front feet in the tire and then take one step over. Once she mastered that, I praised her, and gave her a break. Then she did two steps in the tire and stopped. Again I praised her for getting a little bit closer to the goal. Before long, she had enough confidence to circle the tire without stumbling or stepping out. And she trusted me enough to know that if she failed, I would not punish her. Only then did I climb in the saddle and lead her through the process.

The most important lesson I learned was how to listen to what Nava Rose needed. I had to understand her needs first, not just command her to obey me. Once I understood, she had a greater ability and desire to obey.

John Wooden, the famed basketball coach from UCLA, used to tell his teams, "Run but don't hurry." That's another lesson Nava Rose taught me. I wasted days trying to get her to master the tire maneuver all in one bite. Once I broke it into small pieces, the training went quickly. Being deliberate, and taking enough time to listen, ended up being both more efficient and more effective.

Nava Rose and I went on to win a national championship. But her story didn't end well, and that's one last lesson she taught me. Not long after we won the championship, she was sent to work with another trainer. I was headed to Penn State University that fall and wouldn't be able to work her. I went along with her to the new trainer for a month, to ease the transition.

That new trainer did something to Nava Rose that I have never forgotten. To get a smooth ride on a horse, it's best if the horse learns how to keep its head down. So this trainer had poured a block of cement out in a pasture, and set a ring in the center of the cement. He took a short rope, and tied one end to Nava Rose's head, and the other end to the ring, and left her there for a couple of weeks, so that she would never want to lift her head again. When I saw that, it broke my heart. Here was a champion horse, and they took the spirit right out of her. She went on to win more awards, but was never the same. She was broken inside.

Top Cat was broken inside as well, when I first met him. I was in my forties by then, and for almost three decades had been building on the lessons Nava Rose taught me. One day I received a call from a woman who had a horse she wanted me to train. I don't usually train for the general public—usually I work for friends or colleagues that I've known for a long time. But this woman was persistent, so I asked her to tell me a bit about the horse.

"He's a bit explosive," she said.

"Can you expand on that?" I asked. "What exactly does he do?"

"Well," she said, "when you saddle him, he tries to throw himself backward, and when you tie him, he pulls back and goes out of control."

A group of teenagers was coming up to the ranch for a weeklong retreat, and I knew that a horse like that would grab their attention. So I said to Top Cat's owner, "You can bring him up on three conditions. One is that you come and stay the week and see how he is being trained. Two is that I make no promises. And three is that I'll train him in front of an audience."

She agreed and brought him up for the retreat. Over that week, Top Cat and I got to know each other very well. He was a Quarter Horse, with a red coat and brown mane and tail, built more like a racehorse than a cow-working horse. He'd been put on the fast track during his training, and in the beginning did quite well. But the training went too quickly, with no time for him to build the trust or emotional stability needed for long-term success. As a result, he was wound up tight on the inside.

When I entered the training arena, Top Cat panicked anytime I got near him. He spooked easily and ran from me, and his whole body shook with pent-up emotion. His main problem was fear. In his early training, Top Cat learned that any failure led to punishment. If he didn't live up to his trainer's expectations, he was tied up and forced to obey. His only option was to fight back.

"What he needs," I told the crowd of teenagers watching us, "is to learn how to handle his fear, how to deal with his pain, and how to have hope."

That sounded great in theory, but it's not easy for a horse, or a person, to do. The pains and disappointments of the past leave deep scars. Those scars can't be overcome by wishful thinking or platitudes.

One of the lines I heard over and over in churches while growing up was "Let go, and let God." The idea was, that when faced with a conflict or crisis, the best course of action was to quit worrying and ask God to sort things out. That sounds all well and good, but no one ever explained exactly how to let go of my troubles.

With Top Cat, I started very slowly. I put a long rope on him, and pulled on it gently to make him move. My goal was to entice him to give in to the pressure and come to me. If he panicked and bolted, I eased up on the rope, and let him run.

Once he calmed down, I started over.

One small step at a time, he learned to trust again. Once he was able to respond to pressure on the rope and come to me, we went a little bit further. I wrapped the rope around him, pulled it gently, and rewarded Top Cat when he came to me and then stood still. Eventually, I could spook him and though Top Cat would want to run, he moved his feet but didn't flee. Step by step, he learned how to respond to fear, rather than panicking from fear. When he failed, I waited patiently and didn't punish him.

After several days of training, I brought out a saddle. As soon as Top Cat saw it, he tensed up, holding his breath and preparing to blow up his sides so he would be hard to saddle. When I gently placed the saddle on his back, he had enough faith in me to stand his ground. As I brought the girth of the saddle up to his belly, he tensed up and held his breath, ready to explode. Instead of tightening the girth, however, I released it. I did this again and again, holding the girth against his belly until Top Cat breathed a sigh of relief. Then I'd reward that small step of faith by letting up on the pressure. It got so that I could saddle and girth him and Top Cat would stay still. I could almost hear the thoughts inside his head: *I don't have to panic—he is not going to punish me.*

In the end, I even taught him to lie down. That was a struggle. For three hours he fought with me until we were both wringing wet. Again, I didn't force him, or punish him, or strike out in anger. Instead, I put firm and steady pressure on him until he gave in and discovered the release of pressure.

When he lay down, Top Cat groaned and groaned. "They treated me so miserably," he seemed to say. "My life is so terrible." As we worked that through, I won his confidence, and he learned to exhale those emotions of anger and hurt.

At the end of the week, Top Cat's owner did something that stunned me. "This horse needs to be yours," she said. Afterwards she turned Top Cat over to me. In return, I gave her one of my "want to" horses, a quiet, gentle creature who was a pleasure to ride. Top Cat, who came to us as a frightened, damaged horse, became a faithful companion. He and I worked together for years, traveling across the country giving Sermon on the Mount demonstrations.

He became, to me at least, a walking miracle. His life was transformed, not in the blinking of an eye, but by a series of small steps of faith—everyday miracles.

That's what we hope to accomplish with Sermon on the Mount. We travel the country planting the seeds for miracles— teaching people how their lives can be transformed, one step at a time. And I'd like to invite you to come along with us. Whether you are a parent or a preacher, a boss or an employee; whether you are a person of faith or someone who doubts that God exists, there's something here for everyone.

We'll go on a journey, learning how to sow faith and trust step by step, so that when a storm comes, or you get caught in a barbed-wire fence, you'll have everything you need to find the way out.

So come along for the ride.

CHAPTER 2

LEARNING THE CRAFT

When I was seven years old, my mother got remarried.

And that, more than anything else, is how I ended up as a horse trainer.

In fact, if life had worked out the way my parents planned, I'd have spent most of my life as a dairy farmer, not a horse trainer. But life, as most of us are too well aware, never quite works out the way we planned.

I was born in 1952, and grew up on the Fruitful Manor, our family's dairy farm in Carlisle, Pennsylvania, just outside of Harrisburg. My grandfather had started the farm, and passed it to my dad. We had about 100 cows, housed on the ground floor of an old white bank-style barn, with a hayloft above, along with pigs and chickens in out-buildings.

I was the youngest of five children. Kathleen was the

oldest, followed by Bob, Priscilla, and David. And from early on, we helped out with milking and feeding and mucking out and the dozens of other jobs it takes to keep a farm going.

Our farm was a small but growing operation. Robert Sterrett, my dad, who also taught agriculture at the local high school, had great dreams for the farm. He kept meticulous records, and was always on the look-out for the latest innovations to make the farm more productive.

Like today, there wasn't a lot of money in farming, so with five growing children to feed, my dad supplemented our dairy production by raising all kinds of fruits. We grew apricots, blackberries, cherries, raspberries, plums, apples, and grapes on the farm, and there was always work to be done.

I loved being on the farm, even from an early age. At the center of everything was my dad. And not just on our farm.

He was a pillar in the community as well. Most of our neighbors also had small farms, so none of them could afford to hire help to harvest crops in the fall. So they all worked together in the fields at harvest time. Afterwards, our neighbors often ended up back at our house for a dinner of barbecued chicken and lemonade and potato salad and laughter. We had a number of relatives who also seemed to find their way to the farm.

Most of what I know about my dad comes from talking with my mother, my brothers and sisters, and other relatives, or is gleaned from looking through his files and old family photo albums.

I know he had a great sense of humor. He and his brothers and their dad were always playing tricks on one another.

He was also a diabetic. This was in the days when treatment for diabetes was less sophisticated than it is today. He had to give himself regular shots of insulin, like people do nowadays. But he didn't have the modern testing equipment of today to keep a close eye on his blood sugar.

When his blood sugar went down, my dad was liable to do all sorts of funny things. Like the time he left my grandfather by the side of the road.

They had gone out on a road trip, and my dad hadn't been careful about what he was eating. And sure enough, his blood sugar got out of whack. Unfortunately, my dad was driving at the time. So to my grandfather's horror, my dad started weaving in and out of his line, as if he were drunk. Thankfully, there was little traffic, so he didn't crash into any oncoming vehicles.

My grandfather knew what was happening, and he kept his head.

"Bob," he said, keeping a calm tone to his voice, "I think you had better let me drive."

"All right," said my dad, and pulled over.

But when my grandfather opened his door and got out of the car, my dad slammed on the accelerator and took off down the road.

He stopped a ways down the road, and sat there, with the

engine idling, as my grandfather hurried after him. As soon as my grandfather got within a few feet of the car, off my dad went again, leaving him huffing and puffing in the dust.

This went on for about a mile, with my dad cackling with laughter every time he took off. Finally my grandfather caught up to him long enough to give my dad a candy bar, and he came to his senses.

At that point, I think my grandfather probably wanted to leave him by the side of the road.

But he didn't.

He climbed in the car, they had a good laugh together, and that was the end of that. That was the kind of humor they had. Always pulling stunts like that on each other.

I treasure those stories about my dad, probably because my own memories of him are so few. Mostly I have bits and pieces, impressions or images of being with him, not complete memories. Like sitting on his lap when he drove our Ford tractor on the farm. Or of him carrying me around when I was just three or four, as he visited with neighbors during one of those chicken barbecues.

One fall day in 1957, my dad took the Ford tractor over to our neighbors, Ruth and Craig Fulton, to help with a corn harvest. It was a tricycle-style tractor—two big wheels in the back, set wide apart, and two small wheels in front, right next to each other. That made it very maneuverable and versatile, but also easy to tip over.

To help with the harvest, my dad planned to attach the tractor to a corn picker, a heavy piece of farm equipment. As he backed up to the picker, something went terribly wrong. No one really knows what happened. Maybe my dad was in a hurry, or was distracted, or just made one wrong move.

All we know is that the tractor flipped over and landed on my dad, crushing his chest and pinning him to the ground.

There were two other men around, and somehow they managed to lever the tractor off of him. But it was too late. Today, with the advances in medicine, and with emergency paramedics who fly in helicopters, maybe he would have been saved.

In 1957, however, there was no hope. First they had to find a phone to call for help—there were no cell phones—and then wait for almost an hour for an ambulance to arrive, followed by the long ride back to the hospital, where he was pronounced dead.

What I remember most in the days following my dad's death was a profound sense of loss, of being adrift or shipwrecked, tossed overboard in a storm.

Because my dad was at the center of everything, when he was gone, things fell apart quickly. My mother was an intelligent, capable woman, but she'd always deferred to my dad. He ran the family business, and she took care of the family home. With five kids, that was a tall order.

But it meant that when my dad was gone, my mother

couldn't manage the farm on her own. So we auctioned off our dairy cows and rented out the fields. My mother brought in chickens that she could raise and sell, so we'd at least have some income.

Our neighbors, who had loved my dad, watched out for us. One of them. a grocer, would keep his eyes out for good deals, and set them aside for my mother. Another helped my mother with the auction, and made sure she got a good deal.

Still, without dad's teaching salary, and with little money coming in from the farm, it was a struggle for my mother to make ends meet.

Sometimes at night I sat at the top of the stairs and listened to my mother weeping as she sat in her chair reading her Bible. She wept for my dad, and for herself, and her children. I knew she worried about money all the time. Once, when the sound of her tears woke me, I broke open my piggy bank and brought her down the few dollars I had, so that she could stop worrying, at least for one night.

The British writer, C. S. Lewis, who married late in life, only to lose his wife to cancer, talked about the hopelessness that comes in grief. "No one ever told me that grief felt so like fear," he wrote.

I think that's what my mother felt. She was afraid and alone, and overwhelmed with all that life had thrown at her.

So feeling trapped and fearful, my mother did what a lot of grieving people do. She looked for a lifeline, a way out of the depths of pain and loneliness.

That's why she turned to the man who would become my stepdad. He was a school teacher, like my dad had been. And he was also grieving, left to raise four children alone when his wife died.

And so two years after my dad died, my mother remarried.

What seemed like a reasonable solution was not an easy match. They were both still on the rebound, and so had unrealistic expectations, hoping this new relationship would compensate for the sorrow and loss they felt. Grief was not a strong foundation on which to build their new marriage.

To top it off, there were now nine children in the house. Blending two large families worked in films like *Yours, Mine, and Ours*, or on television, like in *The Brady Bunch*. But it did not work for the Sterrett-Berrys.

We'd had a big family up till that point, but now it was huge. I had three new brothers—Jim, David, and Ken—and a new baby sister, Jeannie. In my biological family, I'd been the youngest, and the apple of my mother's eye, but when Jeannie came on the scene, all of a sudden she was the baby of the family, and I lost my place in the sun.

Bringing three new boys in the house brought more tension as well. We didn't get along, which was to be expected, given all the change in our lives. But rather than helping us work through those difficulties, and learn to get along, the parents took sides. My mother was on our side; my stepdad took the side of his children.

The main problem was this: our stepdad could never fill my dad's shoes. They were two different people—while my dad had been an extrovert, an energetic man who loved people and loved working outdoors, my stepdad was more passive and bookish, and often withdrawn.

He'd come home and want to grade papers, and then read and relax; whereas my dad had been in constant motion, coming home from work and launching himself into farm chores.

My stepdad and I never got along when I was growing up. I don't think I could forgive him for not being my dad. As far as I could tell, we were a mystery to him. He didn't know how to connect with these new children he'd inherited, and so he withdrew.

People get angry when they run out of answers, when the problems they face seem overwhelming. That's what happened to my stepfather. He withdrew, and tried to ignore the troubles in the house, hoping they would go away. But if we kids got into fights, or were disobedient, he'd either become very passive and hide or explode in rage. I just don't think he knew what to do with us.

My mother was sad and lonely, even after the marriage. I remember that at times, when it was so hard to keep peace in the house with the children, and hard to make the finances work, and to have hope that things would get better, I'd still find my mother sitting in the living-room, reading her Bible, and weeping in the middle of the night.

The one thing that kept me going was that I had a great tenderness in my heart toward my mother. She always tried to stand up for us, and reward us when we did well. When we disobeyed, she tried to be firm and fair. When I deserved it, she spanked me, and sent me to my room. But she didn't leave me there for too long.

Whenever I was sent to my room, all the anger and disappointment would stir up inside me. Every child is angry and cries when they are punished, and feels as if they have been treated unfairly. For me, those feelings were intensified by the disappointment and anger that were always hanging in the air. I didn't know what to do with these feelings.

So after I cried for a while, my mother would come and see me. She didn't say anything. Instead, she'd sit on a chair or at the end of my bed, and before long my heart would melt, and I'd let all those emotions out. I wouldn't be the man I am today without my mother's persistent care for me. She never let me get bitter, and always reminded me that even though she didn't always like what I did, she loved me.

Around this time, my parents made another decision that changed my life.

They decided to take us on a family outing to the South Mountain Fair in Arendtsville, about twenty miles from our home.

The idea of spending the whole day pretending that we were having a good time had no appeal for me. Not even the promise of a chicken dinner at the end of the fair held any appeal.

After wandering around seeing the prize pigs and cows, we made our way to the horse arena. A local 4-H drill team was putting on a show that afternoon. As we sat there on the bleachers, in came this brilliantly colored drill team, all dressed in green and white, and riding in perfect unison.

They looked like they were having the time of their lives, riding their horses in pinwheels and spirals and crossing patterns, keeping time to the music.

When the music sped up, the team sped up, cantering and galloping through their maneuvers, to the delight of the crowd. As soon as they finished, I said to my mother, "I want to be a part of that."

Although we lived on a farm, I'd spent very little time around horses. My sister had a big white horse, but I'd never showed much interest. But seeing that team perform together captured my imagination. I wanted to be part of something like that.

So at the beginning, my interest in horses had nothing to do with horses. That changed later on, as I came to love my horses, and invest my life in them. What I wanted was a relationship and connection.

That's an important point to make. There's this mystique that surrounds trainers who work with troubled horses, or who use the methods known as horse whispering. The name itself is misleading—I don't whisper to horses, I listen to them more than anything.

But there's the idea that being a horse whisperer is a kind of mystical gift some trainers are born with. It's as if we have this ability to connect with horses on a spiritual level that other trainers don't have.

Now some trainers do have an innate ability to work with horses. I got my first paying job as a horse trainer when I was fourteen, working with a pony named Colonel Ted, so I had some natural talent as a trainer.

But the techniques I use didn't come from some mystical source. I learned them because I wanted to know what makes a horse tick. First for selfish reasons—I wanted to be part of a drill team, to perform and win medals, to build up my self-esteem and create a sense of belonging. And later, because I wanted to be partners with a horse, so we would both benefit. When I stopped looking at my own needs and began to think about his, things really took off.

But it was never easy. In fact, my first attempt to train a horse ended in disaster.

Not long after coming home from the South Mountain Fair, I purchased a black pony by the name of Scotty. He was old and stubborn, but he was mine, so from the first time we put him in a pasture at our house, I started dreaming of being a champion 4-H rider.

There was just one problem. Riding in a 4-H drill squad is about teamwork, with each horse and rider working in unison. I suppose it's a lot like the marching bands you see at college football games during half time, where dozens of musicians march in perfect unison and create intricate patterns, all in perfect step. It only works if everyone does his job, and is in the right place at the right time.

Scotty, however, had no interest in working as a team. He was a little older, and had developed some bad habits. Whenever I would climb into the saddle, he'd want to take off towards the fence, and then race along the fence-posts, ignoring the directions I gave with the reins. I held on tight until he'd had his fun, and then he was willing to listen.

At eight, I didn't have the strength or experience to know how to guide Scotty. He never tried to hurt me, so I am grateful for that, but trying to join the 4-H team with Scotty would have been a lost cause.

Scotty was too clever for his own good.

We didn't chain the gate of his pen at night. One night, about a year after I had gotten him, Scotty started playing with the latch which held the gate closed. Before too long he had gotten the gate open. He bolted, taking my sister's white horse Topper along with him. It was late at night, with no street lights out in the country along the road that ran by our farm.

Scotty and my sister's horse ran down the farm lane and

across the highway, where a milk truck was passing by. The driver saw the white horse, who was faster than Scotty and took the lead as they ran. In the pitch dark, however, he didn't see Scotty, and hit him, killing him instantly.

My dream of being a champion rider was turning into a nightmare.

One thing you learn early on the farm is that death is a normal part of life. As an eight-year-old, no one blamed me for the accident, although we did learn to latch and chain our gates from that point on.

A few months later, I was climbing into the cab of a box van truck, headed to my first 4-H meeting. In the trailer behind the truck was a sixteen-hand, red-and-white Paint Horse named Cochise. He was part Draft Horse, so he was huge. But he was quiet and gentle, and easy to ride, much easier than Scotty had ever been. Because I was so short, getting in the saddle was a challenge. I had to get a stool and climb him like I was climbing a tree.

I was literally the peanut riding the elephant—that's how I looked when I rode off to join the drill team. The other riders had a good laugh when I started, but Cochise worked well, and soon we were a valid part of the team.

We call an older, well-trained horse like Cochise a babysitter. You can put a small child on him, and if they fall off, the horse will just stand there with his foot up until the child can crawl away—he will not step on that child. He won't mind being climbed on, and he will wait patiently, until the child shimmies up on his back, no matter how long it takes.

Sitting in the cab, with Cochise, I was riding into a whole new world.

CHAPTER 3

ANYTHING WORTH DOING IS WORTH DOING POORLY

SUCCESS IN LIFE IS A GIFT, says bestselling author Malcolm Gladwell, in his book *Outliers*.

It takes lots of hard work, but that's only part of the picture. The other part is having the opportunities that make the hard work pay off. We can only succeed, he argues, with the help of other people, who create the circumstances that allow us to grow and develop.

Take someone like Bill Gates, one of the founders of Microsoft. Now one of the richest men in the world, he spent thousands of hours as a school kid learning how to program computers. That hard work gave him the skills he needed to become a brilliant programmer and innovator.

But Gates was also given opportunities. In the late 1960s,

he attended Lakeside School in Seattle, one of the first schools in America to have access to a computer network. The only reason the school had access to computers was that parents at the school raised enough money to pay for it. In other words, those parents made space for Gates to succeed.

I'm not a genius like Bill Gates, just an honest cowboy. But I know that any success I have in life, I owe to the many people who invested their lives in me when I was growing up. I stand on their shoulders.

As we get older, it's difficult to remember this. The temptation is to think that we are somehow like the Lone Ranger, or Clint Eastwood, or any one of the dozens of heroes of old cowboy movies or modern-day action films, where the lone hero saves the day.

Because of this, we get impatient with other people, when they fail to live up to our expectations. Maybe it's a child who just can't seem to figure out how to get the right answers in his math homework, or a clerk in the store who's having trouble with the cash register, or an employee who keeps messing things up, no matter how many times we lecture him on the right way to do things.

I've had some success in my life. As a teenager, I won several national 4-H titles as a rider and trainer, and by the time I'd graduated from high school I had a room full of trophies and ribbons I'd won. While I was a student at Penn State University, I was elected president of the Block and

Bridle Club, one of the largest student groups on campus, and also as the student representative to the faculty senate for the school of agriculture. My professors offered me a job on campus and allowed me to bring horses to train on my own while I studied. After I finished my bachelor's degree, schools like Ohio State, Colorado State, and Florida State offered me assistantships, so I could go on and earn a master's degree. (I turned them down, but that's a story for a little later on.)

When I was just out of college, one of the largest horse breed associations in the country offered to bring me in as the successor to their president, so he could train me in his job and then I could take over when he retired. Today, I run a well-respected camp and youth training program, and am invited to speak all over the country.

I don't say all of this to brag, but to make a point. It's easy to forget where I came from. It's easy to forget that when I started out, I was an eight-year-old kid, desperate to hang onto the saddle, with no clue what I was doing. I was no one special, just an ordinary farm kid.

Thankfully, when I showed up to join the 4-H drill team, no one laughed me off the rodeo grounds. Despite my looking like a peanut riding on an elephant's back, the rest of the team accepted me. So did the adult leaders of 4-H, who spent countless hours driving us to events, leading our meetings, investing untold hours of their time with us.

One of the first leaders was a woman named Mrs. Dubs, a neighbor who was a widow. Mrs. Dubs was a chain smoker and was considered rough around the edges. That was quite a change for me, as I grew up in a strict Christian household, where my mother was like white on rice about going to church and avoiding any vices. But my parents knew that Mrs. Dubs and the other 4-H leaders cared about me, and so they trusted them enough to let me spend time with them.

At one point, I was elected to become the news reporter for our club. That meant putting together an end of year report on all our accomplishments. Instead of simply typing up a report, I wanted to do something special. So I designed a scrapbook in the shape of a clover-leaf, the symbol of 4-H. Mrs. Dubs offered to help me complete the project.

Before long I realized that there is a reason most scrapbooks are square. Making one in the shape a clover-leaf meant that every page had to fit that pattern. I spent three solid days at Mrs. Dubs' house working on that project. She fed me and put me up and stayed up until the long hours of the night. She offered suggestions, and encouraged me to keep going when I wanted to give up.

Now a scrapbook, I admit, sounds like a small thing. And the easy thing for Mrs. Dubs to do would have been to tell me that a clover-leaf scrapbook was impractical and not worth three days of effort. Instead she stuck with me. She made me feel important; that my ideas mattered.

That scrapbook got me noticed by people in the 4-H organization. It won an award, because the 4-H officials realized it wasn't a run-of-the-mill report, and it opened up doors for me to do other projects in the future.

Then there was George Zimmerman, a local businessman who had a lot of horses. He gave me my first real job as a trainer, when I was still a teenager. Not only did he give me a job, but he bought horses costing many thousands of dollars for me to work and believed that I could train them well enough to increase their value. Once, he and I flew from Pennsylvania all the way out to Albuquerque, New Mexico, to see one of the horses we'd trained run in a race.

Jim Gallagher, an extension specialist for Penn State, took an early interest in me because I was from his county. He opened the door for me to take some of the horses I was working with to the Penn State campus, to train them while I was going to school. He even found a job for me in the horse barn, which took care of my room and board.

The point is this: I didn't get to where I am today on my own, simply by my own skills and effort. I got there because people believed in me, and offered me a chance, even when I was young and unskilled, and made mistakes. Without their help, without their belief in me, I wouldn't be where I am today.

I also owe a great deal to Cochise. He was the perfect horse for me to start with.

He was well trained and responsive; what I call a "want to" horse. That is, he wanted to do what his rider asked him to do. He wanted to be cooperative, and was easy-going, and was responsive to a rider's cues.

So as I started practicing with the drill team, being on Cochise made things very easy. Though I had a lot to learn, I knew that I could trust Cochise to do whatever I asked of him. When I wanted him to speed up, he sped up. When I wanted him to go right, he went right. That put my mind at ease, and while I was on the saddle, my mind could be totally focused on learning the patterns and intricate teamwork required in the drills.

Horses aren't dumb, and Cochise knew that there was no way I could force him to do what I wanted. I didn't have the strength to control him if he wanted to ride off and ignore my directions.

Because he was part work horse, I didn't expect him to be so nimble and athletic. But he made me feel like a champion in the saddle, because we worked flawlessly together.

Scotty, my first horse, had been the exact opposite. He was a "have to" horse, who did what he was asked only when a rider was experienced or strong enough to force him to obey. If I'd taken him to the drill team, it would have been a train-wreck of a disaster. I could force him to do what I wanted, if I concentrated. But it was always a battle.

The same thing would have been true of Skeeter, another horse I trained early on. She was a better horse than Cochise, when it came to her physical attributes. A dark bay Quarter Horse with a black mane and tail, she looked very pretty. She'd been raised out West and had been a ranch horse before I worked with her. I thought she was a real cowboy's horse, and I looked great riding on her in the arena.

That is, until she bucked me off.

Almost every time I rode her, Skeeter would eventually throw me out of the saddle. The problem was this—she was talented but flighty and insecure. She'd been rushed in her early training and as a result was fearful and reactionary. I didn't know how to conquer her fear and so I suffered the consequences.

I stuck with Skeeter for a while, in part because I was too stupid to help her and too stubborn to quit. More than that, I wanted to figure her out.

These two horses, Skeeter and Scotty, perplexed me. They were athletic and talented horses, and so should have been able to run circles around a horse like Cochise. They were small enough that I could force them to do what I wanted, but it was always a struggle.

Cochise, on the other hand, a horse who I could not control by force, was a willing partner. It was Cochise who first taught me the possibilities of working as a team, where the rider and horse are in perfect sync. Even as I moved on to some faster and more athletic horses as I grew, that first partnership with Cochise remained the model I strived for.

I took those lessons from Cochise into my first training job. When I was about fourteen, and still very rough around the edges, some of my neighbors hired me to train a horse named Colonel Ted.

A little roan pony, he'd been kept in a fenced-in field by his owners, and treated well, but had never been ridden. His owners wanted him halter-broken, which means that I needed to civilize him. He was a friendly horse, with a good nature, but had never learned the basics. Imagine a person who'd never learned how to eat with a knife and fork, or other table manners. That's the kind of thing I had to teach Colonel Ted.

His owners wanted him to be able to take a bridle and saddle without resistance; to learn how to stand still and not run off when a rider was climbing in the saddle; to learn how to walk, canter, and trot. Mostly it was about teaching Colonel Ted to be patient, calm, and confident, so that he wouldn't react or buck or rear when something spooked him, or he saw something unusual.

Put yourself in a horse's shoes for a moment. Imagine you are Colonel Ted, and that for most of your life, you've had it pretty easy. You spend most of the time outside in the sunshine, running around and playing, grazing on sweet grass, and being petted and pampered when your masters come to see you. It's a pretty good life.

Only now, a stranger comes into your happy home and starts bossing you around. And he starts tying all kinds of ropes on you, and pulling you around, and maybe even tries to climb on your back. Even worse, he leads you out of the pasture and toward a trailer. The ramp leading up it is metal and it clanks and makes strange noises when you step on it. And as far as you can see, there's no escape route. I don't know about you, but I'd be pretty nervous the first time that happened. Like most of us, he was scared of change.

Remember too that in the wild, horses are prey animals. And God made them fast, with a flight mechanism, so that when they are startled, their first instinct is to run away as fast as they can. That instinct, honed over millennia, is engrained in the heart of any horse.

So it's no surprise that the first time I approached Colonel Ted's enclosure with a rope in my hand, he took off running, trying to put as much distance between him and myself as possible.

I had two choices when I started working with Colonel Ted. I could have cornered him, clipped on the lead rope and tried to force him to do what I wanted. Since Colonel Ted was pretty good natured, he might not have put up too much of a fight. For some of the trainers I met growing up, that kind of domineering approach was the preferred method. You had to let the horse know who was boss from the beginning.

Even as a teenager, that kind of approach didn't appeal to me. Instead, I set out to win Colonel Ted's trust. That meant going over several times and building enough of a friendship with him so that he would trust me enough to let me get close to him and handle him.

The first thing I did was get close to him, approaching him with a slow, gentle manner, so he wasn't spooked. As I walked toward him, I talked in a quiet voice, so that he allowed me to get close enough to pet him. I spent a few hours with him on my first visit, just getting to know Colonel Ted.

When I came back a second time, I wasn't a stranger. He came to me now, when I walked into the corral. And after an hour or so of talking to him, he was at ease enough for me to put a halter on him, and lead him out of his corral and into our horse trailer, so we could take him to our farm. The plan was for me to work with him there for several months, and once he'd been trained on the basics, his owners would come and get him.

When we got back to our farm, I led Colonel Ted out of our trailer and into the corral, where we could work together. I'd come home from school, and spend the rest of the afternoon working with Colonel Ted. In those afternoons together I taught him all the basics, and eventually was able to put a saddle and blanket on him and ride him.

When he went home to be with his owners, I felt the

satisfaction of a job well done. I was still a teenager, and it felt good to have been paid to train a horse. To my knowledge, he always worked out well for his owners.

Some of the lessons from that first training experience have stuck with me over the years. Most importantly perhaps is this: I learned the power of small successes. That's something many of us forget as we grow older.

Rather than focusing on the result I wanted—having Colonel Ted be a well-trained horse—I had to start with a simple step that was right in front of me, then take one step at a time until we reached the goal.

So step one was getting Colonel Ted used to me, so he wasn't nervous being around me. Then I had to get him to let me pet and handle him, especially around his face, so he wouldn't bolt when I put a halter on him. Then it was asking him to do a simple task, like letting me attach a rope to the halter, and following me as I led him.

We took each task, one at a time, and I praised him at every encounter, so that one success built on top of another. It really was like climbing a set of stairs one step at a time, until after a few months Colonel Ted became a well-trained and useful horse.

As I travel the country talking to people about leadership, and how to be seen as an effective, trustworthy leader—whether it's with horses or people—I constantly try to remember the power that small successes have.

When we have something that's working well, like a perfect touchdown pass thrown in a football game, or a horse performing well in the show ring, or an orchestra playing in perfect harmony, it captures our imagination. We want to be like that player on the field, or the rider, or the musician, who seems to be performing perfectly, almost without struggle or effort.

What we don't see is all the practice and struggle that made the performance possible. When we see the finished product, it captures our attention because it is so fluid and seamless, and in harmony. It has power and rhythm and oneness.

Or we see a great marriage, a couple who love each other dearly and work well together, whose children are well behaved and happy, and we say, "I want that."

Unfortunately, that marriage or those great performances seem out of reach. I get frustrated at times when I see something that I aspire to, something that is good and honorable, but I realize I am absolutely clueless about how to get there.

Take, for example, the great Olympic skaters, with their triple axles, and graceful skating that makes it look like they are dancing on ice. It's breathtaking to watch them.

But what happens when I get on the ice? I fall a lot more than I ever stand up, and quickly become disappointed and angry. I am disillusioned quickly, because the process of learning to skate in a straight line, without falling, is frustrating and time-consuming. Before long, I give up. Or I get angry and take it out on the people around me.

Success in anything—real, lasting, long-term success—takes hard work, and a lot of frustration. It's worth it in the end, when we reach the goal, but the irony is that we reach the future goal by focusing on doing what's right in front of us today.

Malcolm Gladwell, who wrote about people who are considered geniuses in his book *Outliers*, describes something he calls "the rule of 10,000 hours"—that is, to be great in any field takes about 10,000 hours of practice. He uses the examples of musicians like Mozart and the Beatles, musical prodigies who achieved enormous success at very young ages. Most people attribute their skill in creating music to sheer talent.

In the play and film *Amadeus*, an older musician named Antonio Salieri is haunted by Mozart's gifts, which seem almost supernatural. He wonders why God would give such talent to Mozart, who lived, by most accounts, an undisciplined life, filled with women and parties, and not Salieri, with his nose-to-the-grindstone approach.

That's not exactly true, Gladwell says. While Mozart had great talent, Gladwell admits, he also reportedly began practicing three hours a day from the time he was three years old. That kind of intensive practice—of scales and learning to play musical compositions note by note, day by day—gave him the skills necessary to bring his musical genius to life.

And the Beatles? Most of us remember them as mop-topped youths, taking America by storm, and causing young women to scream with joy at their mere appearance.

But before they became overnight sensations in the US in the 1960s, the Beatles spent several years playing in Berlin. They played marathon concerts in small clubs, sometimes playing as much as ten hours per night. In those marathon performance sessions, they honed their talent, and learned the skills that later on would allow them to be great. In some ways, the old saying that "practice makes perfect" has some validity.

Take, for example, the professional football player Junior Seau. In December 2008, the New England Patriots football team was decimated by injuries. Five of their linebackers were placed on the team's injured reserve list, meaning they were out for the season. In desperation, they placed a call to Junior Seau, a former star who had retired at the end of the previous season, intending to spend his time surfing and playing with his kids. When he left the game, Seau, who was nearly forty, was one of the most celebrated football players ever, credited with more tackles than any other player in the league's history.

A few weeks after he rejoined the team, a television program visited the Patriots and filmed their practice. There in the middle of the field was Seau, running the same drills as the greenest rookie player.

"You see this," the coach said, pointing to Seau. "All-time leader in the history of football, doing tackling drills."

Not everyone who practices 10,000 hours will become a superstar. But to become successful at anything requires painstaking effort, doing the little things over and over again until they become second nature.

That's not the recipe for a get-rich scheme or a pain-free road to an easy life. That kind of work transforms your life, and can allow you to achieve things you only dreamed about.

Forgetting those lessons, and trying to take short cuts, eventually leads to frustration. That's why my two horses, named Seaweed Sue and Nava Rose, are engrained in my mind.

I bought Seaweed Sue when I was a teenager, spending all my savings to pay for her. A Quarter Horse, she was the most beautiful horse I'd ever seen at that point, dappled gray and well conformed, a huge contrast to Cochise. He was a work horse, she was a racer. He was steady and dependable, she was full of energy and excitement.

By that time, I was a more experienced rider, ready for more speed and more excitement. So we were well matched.

Because she was fast, Seaweed Sue and I could do more complex athletic events, like barrel racing and pole bending. In barrel racing, the horse and rider gallop round a series of barrels, patterned in the arena. You race in at full speed, circle a barrel, race to the next barrel, circle it and then hurry to the next. When you've successfully run around each barrel, the horse and rider race to the end point, trying to finish the course in the least amount of time, without upsetting any barrels.

Pole bending, on the other hand, resembles slalom skiing, where each contestant weaves in and out between a series of stripped poles, trying to navigate the course as fast as possible.

Seaweed Sue excelled at both contests, and the more we won, the harder and faster I pushed her. That got me the results I wanted, but in the end it wasn't in her best interest.

In fact, the more we won, the more obnoxious she became. The only reason I had any control over her at all was because I rode like a monkey—I just hung on to the saddle as hard as I could while she raced and jumped all over the place, doing a jig and sometimes rearing up on her hind legs as she waited for the race to begin. I controlled her by force, and when I let go of the reins, Seaweed Sue was off and running and I was hanging on for dear life.

What I should have done was stop racing her for a while, and gone back to the basics. Because Seaweed Sue was talented, her training was rushed, so she never built up the maturity and self-confidence of a well-trained horse. Instead, like her previous owners, I put up with her difficult personality because she won, and that's all that mattered to me.

I wanted her to be a champion, and I didn't know what it would take to get there. So while we achieved success, we both learned a series of bad habits along with way. If we'd gone back to the beginning, and built up Seaweed Sue's confidence, she might have achieved even more success. Instead, she taught me how to be a bad trainer, who got his way by force. When she gave me trouble, I yanked her back into line.

That approach, as we saw in Chapter One, didn't work

with Nava Rose. I was trying to teach her a complex task—how to spin in a circle while keeping her feet in a tire—and she just didn't get it. She made me look bad, and it upset me. In response, I threw her to the ground.

The focus was on me. In essence, I was telling Nava Rose, "If you do what I say, that will make me look like a better person. If you don't do what I say, that makes me look bad, so I am going punish you."

In order to teach Nava Rose, I had to forget about me for a while. What she was telling me was, "I'm confused and overwhelmed. Help!"

The worst thing to do in that kind of situation is to freak out, and over react by yelling, or in the case of Nava Rose, getting angry and shoving her. Believe me, people have been trying this from the beginning of time, and yelling at a confused person, or horse, only makes things worse.

If I'd been a better listener, I could have avoided that blowup with Nava Rose. Earlier we talked about the importance of practice, and I believe in the power of practice and hard work.

But it's not just the repetition involved in practice. To make practice effective, you've got to always be observant and listen. The idea is this: to take an honest look at your performance in practice, identify where things are going wrong, and then take small steps to improve.

It wasn't that Nava Rose wasn't practicing hard enough.

The problem we had was that I was focused too much on the end goal—of having her be able to spin in a circle—and not enough on the steps needed to reach that goal.

With Seaweed Sue, the goal had been enough. I was strong enough and stubborn enough to muscle past her flare-ups, and hang on to complete our races.

With Nava Rose, who was learning more difficult tasks, strength and determination were not enough. I had to become smarter.

Sometimes the response is to back off, and break things down into more manageable tasks. More often, the answer is to watch and wait, and trust that practice can make perfect.

Just ask Javier, one of my former students.

I met Javier in the 1970s, when I was teaching at a college in California. He was in his early thirties then, and was going back to school to learn the horse industry. Part of that training included learning to ride horses for the very first time.

I liked Javier. He was quiet and unassuming, but underneath that façade was the best pool player I'd ever met. He would make a bet with you, like you were two friends hanging out, and then bang!—he'd knock in every ball and you'd be forced to admit you'd been suckered. But he was far from horse savvy, and had very little experience. It would have been easy to look at him and conclude that he would never be a horseman.

I spent a year teaching Javier to ride, and watching him

was painful. He would sit rigidly and upright, and despite every attempt to get him to relax, he rode at a trot, bouncing up and down, going *bang, bang, bang, bang, bang* in the saddle.

The key to riding a horse is learning how to relax and flow with the horse. New riders are tempted to grip hard with their knees and hang on the reins, as if they are handlebars on a bike. A good rider instead will relax and breathe, and concentrate on moving in time with the horse.

Unfortunately, Javier was caught in a vicious cycle. He was afraid, and so he hung on as tight as he could and gripped the horse with his knees. But the harder he gripped, the more uncomfortable the horse became, and so the horse moved faster, making Javier more insecure, and so he gripped even tighter.

And the more I tried to force him or yell at him, the worse the cycle got. The best way you can help a person like that is to get their focus on something else, to get them to breathe and relax, and to take small steps of success, until they find their rhythm.

So he'd been riding for a year, and still Javier was bouncing all over the place like a sack of potatoes. It would be easy to lose hope in someone like that and become frustrated and angry with them or yell at them.

For a teacher, a student like that is embarrassing. I started thinking that I'd wasted a whole year working with him, and was tempted to believe there was no use putting any more effort into him.

Then one day, he got it.

We were out in the training arena. All of a sudden, I heard this screaming. At first I thought there had been an accident, and someone had been hurt.

As I looked to see where the screaming came from, Javier rode by, yelling at the top of his lungs, "I got it! I got it! I got it!"

CHAPTER FOUR

GETTING PAST NO

From the moment I saw the trucks pull up, I knew I was in trouble.

We were at a fairground in Georgia, where I was scheduled to do a Sermon on the Mount presentation. A large crowd had gathered, including some influential businessmen, so I was eager to make a good first impression.

The organizers had arranged for several local owners to loan me their horses for the evening. What I'm usually looking for are horses who have never been trained or ridden before, or horses who have had some training, but have run into trouble in the process.

Usually I end up working with horses who have been cared for physically—that is, their owners have kept them well fed and healthy, and sometimes even doted on them with love and affection. But somewhere along the way their training has been neglected, and so the horses haven't reached their full potential.

Sometimes their owners have been too busy, or have felt overwhelmed in the training process. And sometimes life has just gotten in the way, and while the owners had good intentions, things haven't worked out.

When I talked to the organizers ahead of time, everything seemed set. But when I arrived, the arrangements had fallen through, and I had no local horses to work with. The organizers apologized, but I told them not to worry.

"Just get me some horses and I'll make it work," I said, trying to assure them.

A little while later, I went outside of the horse arena to get a little fresh air. All of a sudden, two trucks rolled onto the fairground, one pulling a horse trailer behind it. Emblazoned on the sides of the trucks were the letters "PRCA", which stand for the Professional Rodeo Cowboys Association. Inside the trailer were two big and ornery-looking horses.

I started to get a bad feeling in the pit of my stomach. *I am in for it now,* I thought.

The drivers got out of their trucks, and when they saw me, walked over.

"We're looking for Lew Sterrett," one of them said. "Do you know him?"

My first thought was to say, "Never heard of him." Instead, I replied, "That's me."

"We've got some horses for you," he said, with a smile.

A few minutes later they'd unloaded two professional

bucking horses, who were veterans of the rodeo circuit. These horses, sometimes known as broncos, are often especially bred for bucking. They are strong and athletic, usually with great endurance, able to send their back legs flying and twisting their body in the air over and over again, in hopes of dislodging their rider.

As the riders unloaded the horses and led them into a corral, I did a little bit of advance scouting. The first horse was a twelve-year-old rodeo veteran. He was a big-boned, coarse-haired, jug-headed, red roan bronc.

"Has he ever been ridden?" I asked, trying to sound nonchalant.

"Not for more than eight seconds, a couple of times," one of the drivers said, with a smile. (That's how long a professional bronc rider has to hang on in the rodeo.)

This horse was so long gone from relationships with people that he didn't have a name, just a number. I decided to nickname him "the Widowmaker." A little grim, perhaps, but it seemed to fit his personality.

The other horse was lighter in build, and only three years old, but he was ugly and mean, kind of like a seasoned gang member, covered in tattoos and bad attitude.

Because he was younger, I thought he would be easier to work with, and not have as many bad habits. I decided to call him "the Kid." After the Widowmaker, he'd be a piece of cake. So I decided to work with the older one first.

Plus, I thought—only partly tongue in check—if the Widowmaker killed me, I wouldn't have to worry about this younger horse.

The rest of my afternoon was filled with making preparations. Having the right boundaries in place was step one. The organizers set up a round pen in the middle of the arena, about sixty feet in diameter, and I walked around it, making sure everything was in place.

Whenever I do a presentation, I make sure it is in a controlled environment. This is for my benefit, and for the benefit of the horses. The pen gives the horses space to run, but does not let them get too far away. And it gives me space as well.

In this case, I didn't want to be too close to an explosive bucking horse. If he felt crowded, he'd become afraid and strike out in fear. Getting a hoof upside the head from a bucking horse is not my idea of a good time.

Most people have never been in an enclosed space with a volatile and potentially dangerous animal. But most of us have been in similarly tense situations, with a co-worker, or a spouse, or a business associate, where one false word or wrong move can cause everything to go up in flames.

Maybe you have a co-worker who's talented but bad tempered, and you've got to confront him about a missed deadline, or a project that's gone wrong. Or maybe there's a dispute at home, over finances, or any one of dozens of other tensions that families face these days. Perhaps you've got a neighbor who's hard to get along with, and you've just about hit the wall. Or you're a parent, with a teenager staring you in the face, and saying "No" and daring you to do something about it.

If you've had any of those experiences, then you can imagine how I felt when I walked into the round pen with that bucking horse.

I had an agenda in mind. I had to earn the Widowmaker's trust, and get close enough to ride him, and not just for eight seconds. I had to get him to stand still long enough for me to climb in the saddle, and then ride around the arena without trying to buck me off.

All this on a horse who'd been trained for years to buck off anyone who got close to him! It felt like asking a Hell's Angel to come over and teach Sunday school.

To add to the tension, about 700 or 800 people were watching, and so I also felt vulnerable as I stepped through the gate. My reputation was on the line. A failure could be embarrassing. What would people think if I made an idiot of myself?

Still, I had some advantages over the Widowmaker. Like I said before, we'd be working together in a round pen, so there were definite boundaries. No matter how this horse wanted to ignore me, he couldn't get away. So he was in a place of my choosing, and had to work with me on my terms, not his.

At the same time, there was enough space for both of us to be safe. He could run away if he wanted, by circling around the perimeter of the pen, giving him some sense of control and security. I, on the other hand, could get close enough to make my presence known, using a rope or a flag to motivate him, but not close enough that he could reach me with his hind legs. Having those kinds of safe, firm boundaries has become one of the foundations of my training.

On occasion I've had to work in a smaller pen with a bucking horse like Widowmaker, or in a pen that wasn't strong enough or tall enough to keep him in. In settings like that, the results are never good.

Like the time I showed up to do a one-day presentation, and found that the organizers had set up a pen with panels that were relatively short, and placed several unruly horses inside.

"Are you sure you can keep those horses under control?" I asked, with some doubt in my voice.

"Sure we can," they said.

About an hour later, however, I found myself going with a truck and trailer over to a nearby Wal-Mart parking lot, trying to round up those very horses, before they got into trouble, or got themselves or someone else hurt.

Like many horses, these two runaways had been clever. It hadn't taken them very long to figure out that the panels were on the short side, and a few minutes after being placed in the pen, they jumped the fence and ran off to Wal-Mart. Luckily, we rounded them up without incident, and the program went on with only a slight delay.

There was no chance for my friend the bucking horse to escape this time. The panels were high enough and strong enough to keep him safe and secure, without feeling threatened. Even if he put up a struggle there was little chance of him getting loose.

I had one other advantage when I went to work with the Widowmaker. I had a plan. If I'd gone in and tried to force him to my way of thinking, it would have been a lost cause. He was too strong and too ingrained in his ways for me to do that. Besides, I didn't want to change his behavior.

Instead, I was after something much bigger—his trust and his loyalty. As my mentor Ward Studebaker taught me, with trust and loyalty, I could get a horse to do just about anything.

I first met Ward when I was about nineteen, and newly arrived on the campus of Penn State University. He looked like he'd stepped off the set of a John Wayne movie. Tall and handsome, with an easy smile and an outdoorsman's physique, Ward was every inch a cowboy. Originally a farm boy from Southern Illinois, he'd won a number of awards as a horse trainer before coming to Penn State to manage the university's horse herd. Very quietly, and without a lot of show, he'd become one of the state's most respected horsemen.

There's a story that's told about Ward's early days at Penn State. The university's equine program has long had a reputation for excellence, but the barn operation was out of sorts when he first arrived on campus. The previous horse manager had left a few months early, and in the interim, some things had been let go.

Ward began getting things in order, but before he'd gotten established, he was asked to represent the university at a national competition, using one of their prized horses. Without proper time to prepare, Ward realized it was a bad idea, but his boss insisted, and so he agreed.

As he predicted, the competition was a mess. He finished in last place in his class, embarrassing both himself and the school. When he returned to campus, his boss told him to forget about training, and stick to getting the barn operation running smoothly.

He followed his boss's instructions, and before too long the barn was in order. On the side, however, he took one horse, and began working with it little by little to be ready for the next year.

You can guess what happened at the next year's competition. With time to prepare, Ward won his competition class, besting a national champion in the process. He never boasted about his prowess as a trainer, and seldom competed, but when he did, he almost always won.

By the time I arrived at Penn State, I was full of myself.

My room back home was filled with ribbons and trophies, attesting to my supposed skills as a teenage rider and trainer. I'd also been training horses professionally for several years, and through a special dispensation from Dr. Tom Merritt, head of Penn State's equine program, had gotten permission to bring some Appaloosa horses with me to campus, so I could continue to train them while going to school.

The Appaloosas belonged to my boss, George Zimmerman, who had first hired me when I was around sixteen. George was no saint—definitely not the Sunday school teacher role model that my mother would have hoped for.

But George and I had much in common. We were both hungry to win, to prove ourselves as good horsemen. George would buy expensive horses, in hopes that the more we won in competitions, the more the horses would soar in value.

George owned Appaloosa horses, which is the breed I trained and rode to win my national title. Appaloosas are light horses, usually with spotted skin, white around the eye, and colored coat patterns. They were originally bred by the Nez Perce Indians, and were prized for their speed and endurance.

Because I was talented, but relatively inexperienced, George brought in another trainer, an older man from Texas, to mentor me. This older trainer knew how to win, having trained several champions.

But he was aggressive towards our horses, and sometimes even abusive. He used a large bit and a heavy hand on the horses, as a way of imposing his will. Now there's nothing wrong with a bridle and bit per se; they are effective tools to help guide a horse. But this trainer, like others of his generation, used the bit to coerce horses into doing what he wanted. He'd win competitions, but would leave the horse worse for wear.

At first, I looked up to this trainer, and tried to model myself on him. I was never brutal with horses, but I did always want to show them I was the boss. This led me to focusing on the horse's face when I was training instead of their source of power and drive—the hip.

Training horses is a little bit like teaching a gymnast or ballet dancer. They are tremendous athletes, with God-given strength and agility. But an untrained horse can be clumsy, and won't reach his full potential unless he is trained how to balance and control his body.

The best way to do that is not by jerking him around by the reins. That treatment, in the end, leaves him out of balance. To truly train a horse, the trainer needs to have control of the horse's hips. Once that happens, the horse can gain the same kind of grace that a ballet dancer or gymnast has. A well-trained horse is always under control, never reactionary.

Not long after the new trainer came on the scene, I noticed a change in the behavior of George's horses. They seemed stressed, and ill behaved. One horse in particular really struck me. He was a young horse, whose name I've now forgotten. I'd trained him from an early age, and always found him to be an easygoing horse, who was eager to please.

As his training progressed, however, a change came over him. He was always on edge, as if he were afraid to make a mistake and be punished. There was always a tension in the air around him, and this once easygoing horse turned aggressive, biting other horses, and becoming hard for people to handle.

George and I both knew something was wrong. And before too long, our new trainer decided he'd be happier somewhere else.

I brought his bad habits with me to the horse barn at Penn State. That, and my over-confidence from my earlier successes, made me cocky and arrogant, sure that I knew what I was doing.

Ward decided that I needed to be taken down a notch. He didn't do it in an angry or rude way. Instead he teased me, nicknaming my Appaloosa horses the "happy losers," and wondering out loud if they'd ever amount to anything.

He really did more to put water on my over-confidence than anybody else. Sometimes he'd say things like, "I don't know why you want to stay with those happy losers. You ought to just get out of the horse business entirely. You ought to do something worthwhile with your life. After all, who wants to be a trainer all their life?"

I did, of course. I wanted to be like Ward.

He got more out of his horses than any other trainer I'd ever seen, with far less effort. It was Ward who first taught me the importance of training a horse's hip. That's where all the control is.

It's a bit like this: Picture a ship at sea. Not an ordinary boat, but a battleship or aircraft carrier, or perhaps a luxury cruise ship. The captain controls the ship's direction by spinning the wheel, up on the bridge.

But the wheel doesn't turn the ship. The ship will only turn and respond if the wheel is attached to the rudder at the back of the boat. If the rudder is in good working order, the ship will navigate smoothly. If the rudder is out of order, then it doesn't matter how hard you pull on the wheel. Maybe in a small boat, you can pull the wheel hard enough to move the rudder. But you can't do that on a battleship or an ocean liner.

Ward was trying to teach me that force or intimidation might work on a smaller or less talented horse. But if I really wanted to be a great trainer, and to work with the most talented animals, I needed to learn how to capture a horse's "want to."

Ward did this by rewarding his horses for their successes, and then constantly pushing them to get better. He offered a real partnership, that allowed them to do far more than they could have done on their own. He turned raw, untrained horses into prizewinning athletes.

When I got to Penn State, I thought I knew what I was doing. So the first thing Ward had to do was to show me I wasn't so hot. Then he had to break some of my bad habits, by showing me a better way. Like I said, it took me years to understand what he was up to.

Do you remember the television show called *This Old House*? It documented the renovation of an older property that had fallen into disrepair. (It was the old-school version of modern shows like *Flip This House*.)

The first step in renovating a house is the demolition phase. You've got to tear down the walls and get underneath the surface to look at the framework and foundation. If that's solid and level, then the renovation can continue. Usually, however, when you open up a wall, you find trouble.

For example, take the case of a window that won't open right. The problem might be the window, and you can hammer on the window frame and try to force things back into place. The real problem is more likely to be in the wall, where there may be some rotten boards or studs that have gotten out of place. Or maybe the foundation's not level, and that's thrown everything out of square.

To fix things right, you've got to take care of the problems below the surface. Once those are fixed, you can make progress with the renovation.

That's what Ward did for me. I looked good on the outside, but I didn't have the proper foundation of training habits so I'd never reach my full potential unless he took me down a few notches, until I was ready to learn. Then he showed me a better way, with a firm but gentle hand. I wanted to be a better trainer, and I wanted to do things Ward's way, because he got the results I was after.

I thought of Ward when I got into the round pen with the Widowmaker. He too thought he was hot stuff, and didn't need to pay attention to me. So gently, I began to tear down his defenses.

Being in the round pen was a good start. He couldn't get away from me, nor could he annoy me. The first step was getting him to acknowledge my presence and my authority, that I was someone worth paying attention to. So I sent him around the pen, using a flag on the end of a flexible rod to direct him. I never struck him—instead, by waving the flag in front of him, I got him to change directions.

After we'd done that for a while, I asked him to look at me. I didn't do that with words—I'm not Dr. Doolittle and I can't talk to animals. Instead, I stood patiently hissing to him, and waited for him to turn his head towards me, instead of turning his back on me. As soon as he did that, I turned away, giving him a release.

I should explain a bit here. By standing and looking at him or by waving a flag at the Widowmaker, I was putting very subtle pressure on him. What I wanted was for him to respond to that pressure by looking to me for direction.

Once he did what I asked, once he showed the slightest sign that he was paying attention, I backed off the pressure. A few minutes later, I came back to him, with a little bit more pressure. This time I wanted him to follow me. So I began walking away from him. Doing that piqued his curiosity, and before too long, he was following me around. Again, once he did that, I released the pressure, giving him a reward.

Next was getting him to stand still long enough for me to rub his face and neck. That's a sign of affection among horses, but not a usual activity for bucking broncs.

And so we went on, step by step, for the next two hours.

Not everything went smoothly. Before putting a saddle on him, I wrapped a rope several times around his belly, to simulate the feeling of a saddle and girth. Once I pulled that rope, he began to buck all over the place. But that was no surprise. It's what he'd been trained to do for years.

If I'd given up at that point, and said, "Look, he'll never change. You can't teach an old dog—or horse—new tricks," I'd have missed out on what came next.

But I knew that progress is slow, when you are trying to win the heart of a horse—or a person. You've got to do it one step at a time, and it's often two steps forward and one step back. Sometimes it's even one step forward and two steps back.

Once the Widowmaker got the bucking out of his system, and turned towards me, as if to say, "What do you want me to do?", we moved on. He got used to the ropes and not long afterwards, I had a blanket, and then a saddle on him.

Then I rode him, not for eight seconds, but for at least eight minutes. I could have ridden him for hours if I'd had the time. Not because I'd forced him to do what I wanted—that would have been a lost cause. He'd started out defiant and angry, but when I offered him a relationship, the chance to do something new, he jumped at it.

And what happened to the Kid, the young horse I thought would be a piece of cake? I worked with him the same way for two hours, but he never gave in. He bucked and kicked and seethed at me for two hours.

Now I've worked with several thousand unbroken horses—those who have never been saddled and ridden before. There have been all kinds. Stallions, mares, and geldings. Grizzled broncs, and even mustangs who've been right off the western plains. On a handful of occasions, I've not been able to ride one in the short time of a presentation. This night was one of those times. After two hours of tense, hard work, I told the audience it was time to stop.

"I could work with him for another thirty minutes but thirty minutes, or thirty hours, won't do him any good right now," I said.

The Kid was not ready to change. Most likely, if I'd pushed him, one of us would get hurt. I was tired and so was he. But he wasn't ready for a relationship, wasn't ready to change. And that's all right too. Maybe we'll meet up in the future and have another go round.

Even so, my time with the Kid wasn't wasted. A few days after the event was over, I heard from one of the organizers who told me that there were some teenaged girls in the audience who'd been going through a rough time with their parents.

Being a teenager, especially a teenaged girl, is hard. Halfway between being girls and being women, and filled with emotions they don't always understand, they can be hard to live with. And their relationships with their parents get easily frayed.

Sometimes those emotions get out of hand, and turn into disrespect towards parents, or mean and cruel behavior towards other teens.

That night, as the girls watched the Widowmaker and the Kid, something changed in them. They saw one horse overcome its fear and its difficulties, and start to build a new relationship and new patterns of living. They saw another horse refuse to give up its angry ways and end up alone.

And some of them decided they'd rather be like the Widowmaker than the Kid. They'd rather have positive relationships with their parents and friends than be in conflict all the time. They had what we sometimes call an epiphany—a moment of insight when they saw a new way of doing things.

Neither those girls nor the Widowmaker changed overnight. It's not like I waved a magic wand and turned them into perfect angels. But they started on a different path that night, one filled with possibilities.

CHAPTER 5

GOD AND A GIRL

I THOUGHT I WAS DOING God a favor.

I had no idea that God—and a girl—were going to turn my life upside down.

It was just after my junior year of college, and I'd been trying to figure out what to do with the summer. I had one last semester at Penn State and planned on graduating in the December of 1974.

Grad school would come after that, and I was already working on applications for assistantships. I had planned to stay around the university for the summer, but the job I'd lined up fell through. Now I needed a Plan B.

About a year earlier, I'd started going to church again. I grew up Presbyterian, and had gone to church as a youngster, but had dropped out once I got to high school. At Penn State, however, my faith became real and personal. I started going to church, and eventually was baptized.

Not long afterwards, I began to spend a lot of time with

a young lady from the church. She was a real sweet gal. I began to date her, and started wondering, maybe this gal will be my wife someday.

She started telling me about this camp outside of Erie, called Miracle Mountain Ranch. She'd grown up going to the camp, and later volunteered there. Knowing my interest in horses, she thought that working at the camp might make the perfect summer job for me.

I'd been to church camp when I was young, and hadn't liked it much but I thought I'd give the ranch a try. Besides, I thought jokingly, I would be doing it to earn some points with God. After all, how bad could it be?

About a month before camp started, I went there. My girlfriend, Debbie, and I decided to drive up to the camp for the weekend to meet some of the staff and to see about lining up a summer job for me.

My first impressions were, to be honest, underwhelming. For one thing, the camp was in the middle of nowhere, about an hour south of Erie, and a few miles outside of the small town of Corry, Pennsylvania.

And at first glance, the camp facilities left much to be desired as well. A long drive up a steep mountain road, past a pasture full of grazing cattle, led to the main camp grounds. The camp was modeled after an Old West ranch, with bunkhouses, corrals, a horse barn, a dining hall and an indoor rodeo arena. Along with horses for the campers to ride, there was also a herd of sixty Hereford cattle. All of that gave the camp a real cowboy-like feel.

Still, I was unimpressed. The camp buildings had a worn feel to them, and many were in need of renovations. They were rustic bunkhouses, sided only with red roofing paper.

Then there were the horses. By this time, I'd become somewhat a snob when it came to horses. I was used to training championship Quarter Horses and Appaloosas with expensive bloodlines, who'd cost thousands and who'd been bred for the show ring. They were great athletes, born with style and power, who had the God-given talent to be champions.

Since the camp didn't cater for show horses, it was easy to overlook the quality of the horses that were at the camp. I didn't want to work with dull horses, and Miracle Mountain Ranch had plenty of what I first thought of as average horses.

I was suffering for the Lord, as they say. So if I could bring my talent to the camp and improve some less-than-championship horses, I'd consider it a good deed. Little did I realize that the roles were about to be reversed, and that I was about to learn some life lessons from the horses I'd looked down my nose at.

I spent the first day meeting and greeting the staff, and putting a good face on. But inside, I was miserable and cranky. I wanted to get in my car and go. That first night I lay in bed, restless and unable to sleep.

I'll admit it, I was pretty selfish at this point of my life.

I didn't think about anyone else but myself most of the time, and what I wanted.

Despite arriving with a chip on my shoulder, I was soon disarmed by the warmth of the camp staff, in particular the director Dale Linebaugh, and his wife, Opal. The more I learned about the staff, the more impressed by them I became.

For one thing, they were all volunteers, which meant that not only did they have to work full-time, but they also had to raise their own salaries, through donations from friends and family and churches. The reason they were willing to make that commitment was that they believed in the work the camp was doing. By investing their time and energy in the kids who went to camp, they were doing their part to make the world a better place. For the first time, I began to wonder if there were more important things in life than horses.

And then, there was the camp director's daughter, Melodie. She was tall, dark haired, dark eyed, and beautiful, with a disarming smile. Not only that, she'd grown up riding horses, even before she could walk, and was a talented rider and performer. Maybe this camp wasn't so bad after all!

When I left the camp, I had an offer for a summer job to work in the ranch's horsemanship program. If nothing else, I'd get to see more of Melodie. I naively mentioned that to my girlfriend on the way back to the Penn State campus.

"That Melodie is really something, isn't she?" I told her on the ride home.

As you might guess, our relationship didn't last much longer.

Finally summer rolled around and I was back at the ranch. This was a pretty good deal, I thought. Once I got past my initial snobbery, I realized the camp's horses weren't all that bad. And the job was good. I'd be around horses all day long, and get to work with a great team of people.

I secretly hoped that Melodie would be there as well—but she was working at a camp eight hours away. Despite the distance, a romance blossomed between us.

By the end of that summer, I was hooked and realized that Melodie was the woman I wanted to spend the rest of my life with. Besides her physical attractiveness, we were well matched. We shared a love of God and a love of horses, and our personalities complemented each other.

She was vivacious and bold with her love of God and others, while I was more reserved, happy to be in the barn with the horses all day. My easygoing manner was a good complement to her intensity.

She was also strong enough to stand up to me and tell me when I was wrong. Not by yelling at me or by withdrawing, but by looking me right in the eye and giving me a straightforward, honest response.

There were other reasons to love her as well. As a kid coming from a broken home, I was transfixed by her parents. Now that we've been married for more than thirty years, sometimes Melodie accuses me of marrying her for her dad as much as for her.

Dale and Opal Linebaugh, Melodie's parents, had started the camp in 1963, and by the time I arrived, they were drawing over 1,000 kids during the summer season. Dale was a tall and handsome man, equally at home on the back of a horse as he was preaching in a pulpit. He was the kind of leader who naturally attracted people to him, with a likeable and generous spirit. He was like the dad I'd never known.

Dale was surprisingly affectionate as well. He was then—and remains even today—a hugger, greeting friends and family with warm affection. The first time he hugged me, it startled me. I wasn't used to being hugged and so responded by becoming stiff as a board. Dale kept hugging me, and as the weeks at camp wore on, my stiff exterior began to melt.

Even if we don't like to admit it, most of us crave that kind of physical affection and affirmation. That goes even for cowboys, despite our gruff ways.

It was Dale who began to show me that there were more important things to life than winning in the show ring. Watching him work with guests and staff, and later with volunteers and supporters of the camp, I realized he was beloved and highly respected.

Like Ward Studebaker, he didn't lead with an iron fist. Instead, Dale inspired and empowered people, which made them want to follow. He was a master at finding people's "want to."

I wanted to be like him. Which is why, three years later, I found myself sitting in his office and trying desperately to fill his shoes.

Life was a blur in the weeks and months after I'd met Melodie. At the end of summer, I went back to Penn State, and finished my last semester of studies. But things had changed. Instead of applying to graduate school in equine studies, I was planning to go to seminary and prepare for a life in ministry.

It was a huge, life-altering change. Many of my friends and mentors thought I'd lost my mind. They'd invested time and energy in grooming me to go to graduate school because they believed I had a great future in the horse business. It seemed like I was throwing it all away for a girl.

They were partly right, I suppose. It did seem like I was throwing everything away. And in the weeks and months that followed, I second-guessed myself dozens of times. But in the end, I knew I had made the right choice.

First, my entire identity had been built around horses, and winning in the show ring. That's all I lived for. That's a pretty shaky foundation to build a life on.

But Ward Studebaker had taught me that winning, in the end, didn't matter as much as I thought it did. When he competed, Ward won. But he rarely entered shows, and wasn't all that impressed with himself when he did win.

Ward understood something I was just coming to grips

with. Winning is not everything. In fact, the process of training was more important than the actual competition. The journey is more important than the destination.

Now, if that sounds like motivational speaker mumbo-jumbo, consider this: When I trained horses, we won, but only by running myself and the horses ragged. We would do anything and everything to look good for the few minutes we were before the judges. All we got in the end was a trophy or a blue ribbon, but nothing of lasting value. Sometimes we ended up worse off, because we were exhausted and ill-tempered by the pursuit of winning.

Ward, on the other hand, focused on the process of teaching his horses, building one success on another. Slowly but surely, he was molding them into better horses—stronger, more confident, and more capable. Competitions were like mile markers, to show how far they had progressed. But the goal of training was to make them into better horses, not just to win awards.

He never lost perspective on what he was doing. And his sense of self-worth didn't depend on how well he did in the show ring. I needed to learn that, and the only way for me to do it was to walk away from the show ring for a while.

Secondly, Dale was teaching me the connection between the principles I was learning as a horse trainer and the ability to lead people. I began to realize that horses would shed light on human relationships. That the same dynamics of trust that enabled a horse and trainer to work together applied to people as well.

Though mesmerized by Dale, I knew the ranch was no utopia and I would later learn that all was not well. Running a nonprofit youth camp, relying on small donors, always trying to stretch every penny, can take a toll. But despite the difficulties in the camp, Dale and Opal always responded with grace. I wanted to be that kind of person; the kind who could face difficult times without cracking.

Thirdly, I'd always worked with top-quality horses, and I'd started to believe that they were the only horses worth working with. Over the next decade, while working at the ranch, I learned that even the plainest horses—and the most ordinary of people—are capable of great things.

It would have been easier to stay on the for-profit side of the horse business. It meant making good money, having a nice house, and having the respect of my teachers and mentors.

Working at a ranch meant a lot of heartache and hard times. It meant being poor for many years. There were times when I thought we'd have to close the doors and give up. But there's been great joy as well. Amazingly, we stayed solvent.

Melodie and I also gained something money couldn't buy—a solid foundation for our marriage.

Though I had received much from my family and was loved much, our struggles growing up had left me longing for a sense of stability. My mom's remarriage had been a disaster, and she and my stepdad had long since split up. The rest of the family had splintered as well. My brothers and sisters grew up and went their own way, with extreme values ranging from conservative to liberal.

One sister went off to become a Methodist minister; another married a guy who became a drug dealer. My oldest stepbrother published New Age books and ran New Age and sacred sexuality conferences around the country, while another brother would eventually come to work for me on the ranch.

Marrying Melodie meant I had to establish my own family and values and a solid foundation for my life. If that meant marrying into the family business, well, that was all right with me. My relationship with her and her family meant more than any success I ever had in the show ring.

And the ride has been worth every minute.

Of course, I didn't always feel that way. Many mornings, during my early years at the ranch, I'd wake up and wonder, *What have I gotten myself into?*

The first thing I figured out was how much I needed to learn. I knew about horses, but not much about leading people or about the Bible. So I went off to New York for a year, to study at Nyack Bible College, while Melodie went to work as a nurse at Bryan College in Dayton, Tennessee. We married a year later.

It would prove to be a busy year, with her starting a new job and preparing for a wedding, and me studying for my master's degree.

During the week I'd be in class; on the weekends I'd go to downtown NYC, and hang out in the coffee houses and on street corners, talking to drug addicts and derelicts. I was about as far from horses as a country boy could get.

Once I was done at Nyack, and we were married, I spent two years at a horsemanship college out in California, where I developed a whole new perspective for the future. It was there that I met my friend Javier.

While in California, I worked for a man who was very inconsistent in his leadership style. He would often change his mind midstream, and so the staff never knew what to expect from him. We rarely had a sense of momentum in our program, because as soon as we made any progress, our goals and priorities changed. It gave me practice in following someone who was hard to work for, and taught me what kind of boss I didn't want to be.

By 1977, Dale and Opal had decided to leave the ranch, so Dale could go back to school. He wanted to finish his PhD, which had been a long-term dream.

Once Dale and Opal departed, the board began to rethink the ranch's future. Eventually, they decided that the best course of action was to sell the ranch. Though it looked like the sale would go through, the board could never finalize a deal.

The next two years proved difficult. My brother-in-law served as the interim director once Dale left, but it was a thankless job. Because the board were hoping to sell, they didn't want to invest a great deal of money in improvements to the buildings and the staff were left in limbo, unable to make many changes until the new ownership was in place.

It was a time of confusion and uncertainty, which caused a great deal of stress and resentment to build up among staff members. They soldiered on, keeping the camp programs running at a high level but they were becoming stressed and disillusioned.

When the sale fell through, the board asked Melodie and me to come back and assume the leadership of the camp. I was twenty-four, and in way over my head. Most of the staff had already served for decades. I was a bit intimidated about coming on board and making changes.

To make matters worse, the camp's finances were in bad shape. Just a few years earlier, Dale had fallen out with his original partner in the ministry. It was a difficult separation that resulted in the loss of community support. Before the split, the ranch had drawn over 1,000 campers a summer. Over the next few years, the numbers began to steadily drop. By the time I'd been on the scene for three years, that number had dropped to around 300.

Turning things around required drastic measures, including cutting expenses to the bone. We didn't even have enough money to make a long-distance phone call. Most of the camp buildings were heated by wood, so the staff and I, along with their kids, cut our own firewood from the forests on the campgrounds. I can remember many days in the cold and rain, cutting and splitting logs so we'd have enough wood to keep the buildings heated.

It was miserable. But it turned out to be a good team-building time, and it would lay a foundation for the deeper healing that was needed.

At the same time, we didn't want to wring our hands, and watch the camp continue to decline. Most of the bunkhouses needed renovations and we didn't have the cash to pay for material. Given our financial state, I was hesitant to take a loan to make repairs. The donor base was very small, so there was little possibility of adding more donations in the short run.

Faced with an overwhelming task, I drew a lesson from my early days with Nava Rose. What I needed was to cut the project down into small pieces, and solve those small problems one at a time. Since we needed construction materials, I began to look for buildings, like old barns that needed to be torn down, and ask if we could salvage some of the materials. Sometimes I'd be driving down the road and see people working on an old barn, and I'd pull the truck over, hop out and ask right then and there if we could have the old boards. Soon the staff team was actively involved in the salvage business.

I had no shame, really. But I did have a vision. What the camp needed was a facelift. The buildings were sturdy enough, but they looked too similar to each other. Since we were a horse ranch, I wanted the grounds to have more of an Old West town image, as if you'd just walked on to the set of a John Wayne movie.

Since we couldn't afford to rebuild the bunkhouses, we took a cue from those old movies and put false fronts on the buildings, with front porches. Those old, gray, weathered barn boards gave the feeling of authenticity, like they'd really come from the Old West. We removed the old nails, pounded them out flat, and reused them to attach the boards.

Those boards were usually so old and dirty that our faces and arms would turn completely black in the process. We worked our tails off for three years, trying to create something worthwhile out of a pile of junk boards and rusty, bent nails.

While the camp was getting a face-lift on the outside, the staff were being reworked from the inside out. They were dedicated, hard-working people, who loved the ranch and spent years there, often at great personal cost. Over those years, however, small hurts had been allowed to fester under the surface unresolved. And there were some unfinished loose ends from the years of transition.

On the outside, people were warm and friendly, but that happy exterior hid jealousy, bitterness, and wounded spirits. Nobody can pretend as well as professional Christians. Behind every "bless your heart" were hurt feelings that no one wanted to or knew how to talk about.

Lew's favorite tool for life illustrations: a horse. Desired Spark is a 1997 Quarter Horse stallion.

Life from the view of a...

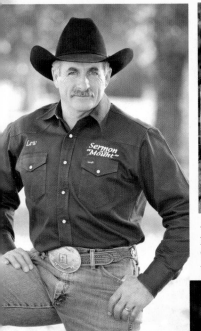

A Horseman – Skip 'N the Spotlite: a 1999 palomino stallion. He is registered both as a Quarter and Paint horse, and is ridden dressage and western seat. His specialty: being a gentleman!

Life in blue jeans: Lew. Dr. Lewis Sterrett, away from the office, podium, and conference center.

A Cowboy – Out for a gallop in Texas on Spark. His specialty: ponying youngsters!

A Trainer – Working with a guest horse on leading and loading. First order of business: building healthy boundaries.

A Man of God – Lew praying with (left to right) Randy Coleman and Charlie Simmons (some of our host crew) before a Plant City, Florida presentation.

Working in multiple venues

Coliseums – State and city-wide campaigns are often hosted in major coliseums. A round pen session at the Will Rogers Coliseum in Ft. Worth, Texas.

All-Terrain – Lew and Rooster's Shalom, a 2004 buckskin Quarter Horse stallion (commonly known as Romeo) discover a small patch of sand.

Indoors is always best, but rain or shine we have gone on since 1981. A leadership training seminar at the Oklahoma State Fairgrounds.

Open lots – An open air forum typically hosted by a group of community organizations in rural settings. Lew on Spark.

On the trail – On the Ranch headquarters in Pennsylvania with guests or students, Lew often takes a break from the arena to teach on the trail.

International travel – Since 2002, this rig has annually traversed a majority of states and provinces in the United States and Canada, making an average of 150 presentations per year.

Training in small steps

Putting protective leg gear on an unhandled horse is a two person job that can prove risky. How they are handled sets the stage for trust or distrust.

PRINCIPLE - BASED TRAINING

Seeing the untrained, fearful horse choose to follow the trainer, rather than avoid him, is a delightful moment for the audience, trainer, and horse.

First saddlings are often met with this reaction. Only a very few buck when Lew mounts a few moments later.

Lew helps a problem horse own and resolve his attitude before he mounts. Graduation presentation at French Camp, Mississippi.

The same horse with 'response-able' training. Everybody wins – the horse, the trainer, and the next generation!

Spark at his best, bridleless and 'mentoring' a young horse for the first saddling and ride.

Lew testing the 'green broke' horse before riding. Featuring Measures of Maturity for a family conference in Big Sandy, Texas.

Results with fruitful outcomes

Discernment – Spark walking through debris of varying natures, obeying Lew's instructions to "come."

Confidence – Romeo being covered by a tarp. The topic – blind faith, or confident trust.

Humility –
Romeo at rest
and seated at the
feet of his master.

Courage –
Romeo's first
walk over a teeter-
totter.

Enjoying "the boys"

Lew with his three stallions (left to right): Spotlite, Romeo, and Spark. Presenting at a men's conference in Colorado on the topic of brotherhood.

Horses love to get out and run, and Spark is no exception. During a photo session, Lew and Spark go for a gallop.

Enjoying some down time on Romeo. Lew has ridden almost every section of the U.S., from the tips of Alaska to Florida.

Training on a brisk winter morning in Texas. Lew saves time by working two horses at once: he rides Romeo to the training corral and returns on Spark.

Time for reflection

Down time is necessary for the horses, too. Fresh grass is always a treat.

Riding together with Melodie has become more of an exception than a rule, but always enjoyed. She grew up riding and training horses on their ranches in New York and Pennsylvania.

After a few months, I realized that someone had to address these conflicts, and since I was the boss, it had to be me. After thinking it over, I decided we'd have a weekly staff morale meeting, every Tuesday morning.

These Tuesday morning meetings became infamous among the staff. First of all, they started out as morning meetings, but soon turned into marathon, all-day sessions.

Not all the problems were caused at the ranch. Some of the staff had come from difficult family backgrounds, and had brought those past hurts with them to the ranch. Those staff members had never developed the skills or confidence to face their hurts and find resolutions.

Some of the time it was like pulling teeth, because no one wanted to be honest. They wanted to put a good face on and pretend things were fine, at least in public.

In the church world, there's this myth that if a leader isn't miserable or living in poverty, then they really aren't spiritual. Ministers and youth workers and camp directors often sacrifice everything for their work—their families, their health, sometimes even their own faith. There's lots of thankless work and little reward, at least on the material side of things.

The ranch staff had somehow come to believe that being poor and depressed was the expected norm. A subtle philosophy had come to be accepted—that the ministry and the camp's programs came first. As long as they were running well, nothing else mattered. So if the staff were bickering behind the scenes, it was all right, as long as they put on fun programs for the campers—as if no one would notice that the staff weren't successful at resolving their own conflicts. But a happy face and a message of God's love don't always cover disharmony and division.

In those Tuesday morning meetings, we began to develop the skills to resolve those conflicts and come to peace.

My father-in-law is a great man, who had the best of intentions. But between the partnership split and living twelve hours away, he was unable to bring about the needed healing. It was my job to make it happen now.

Again, borrowing a page from Nava Rose, I started small. I couldn't start to mend fences with the staff unless they were honest with me. So little by little, as I was honest with them, I began to tease their stories out of them. Much of the time it was not easy to hear or apply these truths about relationships, but they worked.

Paul and Marcia Carlstrom owned a family farm before coming to Miracle Mountain Ranch. They sold their farm and donated most of their equipment to the ranch. They had sacrificed diligently to get the horse-and-cattle program on its feet.

During the transition, it was implied that Paul might eventually be named Director. In order for us to work together, we needed to get past this point.

The Carlstroms lived in an old farmhouse on the camp

grounds, with a cracked foundation that made the house sag in the middle. They'd been promised better housing, but it had never materialized. It would take time for me to make good on those promises.

Another couple lived with their three young children in a travel trailer that had been parked on the grounds. Over the years a small addition had been added on, with a bathroom and living-room, all suspended on wooden posts. But it was no place to raise a family, especially in the bitter Pennsylvania winters. They needed a new place to live.

Once the problems were out in the open, I could go to work on solving them. Part of that process was apologizing to the staff for my own shortcomings, and for anything I'd done which had made matters worse. Then I began to sit down, one on one, to figure out what promises had been made, and what I had to do to make those unfulfilled promises right.

It took years to do that. Some of the staff had decided to leave by then. But some remained and are still with us.

One thing I promised was that I'd always be straightforward with the staff. Once I got a better handle on the housing, I began making plans to do what I could to correct the situations.

"I can't fix this right away," I told the staff. Surprisingly, they weren't angry with my responses. Disappointed, yes, and some decided to leave. But with that straightforward response, I began to earn their trust and respect.

Being a leader often involves disappointing people. It goes with the territory. But honest disappointment beats false hope any day.

While things didn't change overnight, we started to see slow and steady improvement. I knew that I needed to earn their trust.

Sometimes I am asked why I didn't make a clean sweep of things, and start all over with new staff. Making a fresh start might have been easier, given the tension and disrespect that plagued the staff when I arrived.

But it was a shortcut, and I knew it. I could bring in a whole new staff, but unless I changed the way the ranch was run, it was only a matter of time before the new staff were burned out and miserable.

There's an idea floating around Christian leadership circles, borrowed from the corporate world. It goes something like this: Running a business, a church, or a Christian nonprofit organization is like driving a bus. The key to success, according to this approach, is to get the right people on the bus, and toss the wrong people off the bus. Once all the right people are on the bus, everything will run smoothly.

While that is a valid point, it's not the whole answer. I've come to understand that a leader should adapt his methods to the people on his staff. If the people on the bus are miserable, maybe it's time for the leader to change the circumstances. For starters, maybe the bus driver should ask people why they are

GOD AND A GIRL

miserable before giving them the heave-ho. It could be that the bus is the problem, not the people.

Besides, firing people wholesale would have been unethical. These folks had invested their lives in the camp and they deserved a chance to turn things around. And to be honest, it's not like people were beating down the doors to join the staff. If the ranch was to have a future, I needed them as much as they needed me.

Out of this process came the most pivotal decision of my life. I was faced with a fork in the road, and had two clear choices. I could either set my energies, focus, and vision on making the ministry successful, even if it meant burning out the staff in the meantime. Or, I could work to make my staff successful. I could make their success and development my priority, and trust that the results would follow. One is a programmatic model and the other is a relational model. I chose the latter. I had no stomach for burning people out in order to further the ministry.

This philosophy began to change the way I worked with horses as well. Instead of demanding that they conformed to my methods, I began to adapt to their needs and limitations.

What kept me going, even in the difficult days, was the vision I had for the staff. I didn't want a happy staff of people who'd do whatever I said, who'd follow my every direction, and do things just the way I wanted. Instead, I wanted a staff that I could trust.

That vision is a lot like the way I see horses. There's a difference between an obedient horse and a trustworthy horse. An obedient horse will do what you tell them, as long as you are paying attention. But if you lose focus for a moment, or a crisis moment comes up, the horse won't know what to do.

A trustworthy horse will have enough training and experience to know what the right thing to do is, even in a difficult time or crisis.

It's the same with people. I wanted a staff that I could trust and partner with.

It's easier to say, if a horse fails, that it's their fault, and the solution is to get a better horse. And if the staff fail, it's their fault, and the solution is to get a better staff.

Helping a horse or a staff member overcome their failures is hard work. In those early years there were a lot of tears, a lot of loneliness, a lot of sleepless nights. But as the weeks and months went by, I could sense that change was coming.

The funny thing is, we almost didn't make it.

By 1980, three years after I'd become the director, we hit the wall. Our numbers were down, and the stress of trying to turn things around was taking its toll on Melodie and me. Our board of directors could see we had come to the end of our rope and encouraged us to sell. Sitting around a table at a board meeting, they told me it was time to shut down the ranch.

The board wasn't angry with us. If anything, they were disappointed that things were not working out the way they'd hoped. They feared that the stresses of trying to turn the ranch around were starting to fray our marriage.

If the camp shut down, it would be difficult and disappointing. But the board could live with that. What they couldn't live with was the possibility that the camp would come between Melodie and me and ruin our marriage.

"Give me one more year," I said.

I'd been inspired by one of the parables that Jesus told about patience. It's found in the thirteenth chapter of the Gospel of Luke:

> A man had a fig tree, planted in his vineyard, and he went to look for fruit on it, but did not find any.
>
> So he said to the man who took care of the vineyard, 'For three years now I've been coming to look for fruit on this fig tree and haven't found any. Cut it down! Why should it use up the soil?'
>
> 'Sir,' the man replied, 'leave it alone for one more year, and I'll dig around it and fertilize it. If it bears fruit next year, fine! If not, then cut it down.'
>
> (LUKE 13:6–9 NIV)

I'd started to see some improvement in the ranch and wasn't quite ready to quit. The board relented, and said we could stay open one more year. If things didn't get better, they'd shut the camp down and sell off the property.

In some ways, being told the camp was on its last legs sounded like great news to me. It took all the pressure off my back.

For three years, I'd been living with the idea that failure was not an option. I didn't want to let Melodie or her parents down. I was trying to fill her father's shoes, and it was an impossible task. The board lifted that burden off my shoulders. I was free to fail. So we began to take more chances, to try new things, without having to worry about the results.

One of the first things I did was sell off the cattle. Beef prices were up that year, and the profits from the sale would give us some funds to work with and provide much-needed room for the large horse herd. We'd kept the cattle herd mostly because raising cattle had been Dale's dream, and we didn't want to change what he'd started.

As we began to try new ideas, attendance began to rise. Parents would come to us and say the strangest things. "We love to send our kids here, because of your staff," they'd say. "They are so loving and they set a great example for our kids."

I had to stifle a laugh, because on Tuesday mornings we were still fighting. But the conflicts were shorter, and often ended in laughter, because we'd learned to work things through instead of avoiding them.

The outcome that was evident to others was love. Visitors and guests to the camp began to comment on how well the camp staff worked together, and that we seemed to have genuine affection for one another.

I began to make inroads into the community as well. The camp split years earlier had alienated some of our former campers. But with our spruced-up buildings and refreshed staff, campers began to return.

Instead of closing at the end of 1980, we began making plans for the future. Little did we know that all the things we'd been learning would be introduced into a brand-new program that began in 1981. This program would not only involve academics and skill training, but would focus on reaching people's hearts and building the foundation for healthy relationships.

It would also open the door for a new work, called "Sermon on the Mount," which would eventually spread around the world.

CHAPTER 6

OVERCOMING LIMITATIONS

FAST FORWARD SEVEN YEARS. It's now 1987, and by this time, the ranch is experiencing a rebirth. Our summers are full, and we're about to celebrate the ranch's twenty-fifth anniversary. I've also got something new in the works, an idea called "Sermon on the Mount."

When Dale was director of the ranch, he spent nine months of the year on the road, speaking at churches and conferences, trying to raise money to support the ongoing work of the camp. He had a natural gift for speaking to groups of people, and had been trained as a pastor and preacher.

Me, I was a tongue-tied Pennsylvanian Dutchman who was allergic to speaking in front of crowds. I didn't mind talking to guests at the camp, but that was usually as a host where I was welcoming them to the ranch, or making a few housekeeping announcements.

The thought of going out on the road and expecting people to show up at a church meeting or a conference to listen to me speak never crossed my mind in those days. I don't think even I would have shown up to hear me speak.

So imagine my surprise when people were inviting me to be the guest speaker at their events. Only I wasn't going alone. The horses were going with me. And some of the average horses from the ranch, the ones I'd originally thought would never make it, had become the star attractions.

We called the presentations "Sermons on the Mount"—a play on words about Jesus' best-known speech and riding a horse. The idea was pretty straightforward. Working through our difficulties at the camp—along with my horse-training experience—had given me some insight into the way relationships worked, especially the importance of listening and trust. Instead of me standing up for an hour and droning on and on about the principles, my horse would help me bring them to life.

The idea was still ragged around the edges. I used an old Ford pickup and trailer that I'd repainted to take my horses out to do these demonstrations. Neither the rig nor my horses looked like money. But I'd been learning that with horses, like many other areas of life, appearances can be deceiving.

That was one of the first lessons the horses taught me, soon after I arrived at the ranch back in 1974. Since I was in charge of the horsemanship program, I came in a few weeks before the campers arrived for the summer, in order to take stock of the horse herd. There were about seventy of them.

Most of them were older, experienced in being ridden by the campers and relatively safe.

Still, you can never be careful enough with horses. Sometimes a horse that appears to be well trained and responsive can turn explosive and dangerous when startled.

I wanted get a better handle on them, and to sort them by reliability. Before we put our guests on the horses, I wanted to know which were safe for even the youngest of campers, and which ones I needed to keep an eye on, who might cause trouble for inexperienced riders.

In the back of my mind, I was hoping that some of the horses would have the potential for more advanced training. Much to my surprise, I found a number of diamonds in the rough in those first few weeks.

One of the horses that caught my eye was Ribbon, a well-bred Quarter Horse mare with a bright sorrel (reddish-brown) coat. She seemed a better match for the show ring than a summer youth ranch, especially in contrast to some of the other horses.

More typical of the ranch's horses was Peyote, who was, in every sense of the word, an average horse. Average looks, average intelligence, average athleticism, average everything. He was all right for giving riding lessons to young campers but that was about it.

Ribbon was a beautiful horse, with a great deal of talent. If they were in high school, she would have been the prom queen, while Peyote would have been a nobody.

Surely, I thought, Ribbon was capable of doing a lot more than hauling inexperienced campers on trail rides. So as the weeks went by, I began to spend more time with Ribbon, seeing what she was capable of. Despite her talent, however, she was a constant disappointment.

While she was obedient, and would do what I asked her to do, she constantly complained about it. Even when I asked her to do a relatively simple task, she'd pin her ears back or wring her tail—swishing it back and forth in irritation. It was a sign that she was always irritable and unpleasant.

Before too long, it became clear that Ribbon had no interest in being a team player. She did everything with a sour attitude that made her unpleasant to be around. On the outside she was a gorgeous horse, but that beauty was marred by her personality. That attitude kept her from reaching her potential, and instead, limited her to being little better than an easily replaceable and unremarkable lesson horse.

I began to take Ribbon along during our presentations, as she made a great example, especially alongside Peyote. That average horse turned out to be remarkably adept during our training, and he became much more skilled than Ribbon ever was. His attitude, and willingness to be taught, opened the door for his success.

Putting the two together would surprise an audience. They'd see Ribbon and immediately think she was the more accomplished horse, and they'd be surprised by her attitude when I rode her. Her movements were choppy, and she would be constantly complaining. Unlike people, horses are generally transparent with their emotions. When they are ticked off, they'll let you know. And Ribbon—though she would eventually become a reliable horse—was ticked off most of the time.

By contrast, Peyote would ride smoothly and respond to my commands almost without effort. He wasn't great at advanced maneuvers, like a flying lead change—more about that later—but he far exceeded the audience's expectations.

In recent years, the horse-breeding world has begun to catch on to the idea that, when it comes to horses, looks aren't everything. A former student of mine now works for the Waggoner Ranch in Texas, one of the largest horse breeders in the United States.

In the past, they've made most of their money breeding horses for the show ring. But they've discovered an unexpected demand for their ranch horses. Those horses used to be considered less valuable than show horses, mainly based on their physical appearance. The show horses often looked great, but they'd never last a day on a real ranch.

By contrast, some of the less attractive horses know well how to get the job done, a skill that's made them rise in value. In recent years, a whole new market and set of competitions has evolved for the once-underestimated ranch horse.

Working with Ribbon and Peyote, my attitudes about horses began to change as well. When I started at the ranch I was a horse snob, more impressed by a horse's looks and breeding than by their attitude. The more time I spent with the ranch horses, the more I realized that a horse's heart and attitude mattered more than their pedigree and their bloodlines.

The horses also taught me more about myself. On the inside, I wasn't much different than Ribbon. My success in training had given me a big head, and I thought I was too important to work with inferior horses. Only the best would do for me. I was becoming a bit of a prima donna, and treated people and horses based on their abilities and outward appearance.

But in the rustic surroundings of the ranch, I began to wonder if I'd gotten it all wrong. Those early years of running the ranch humbled me. I was no longer the hotshot, horse-training college kid I'd been when I first arrived. Turning the camp around had tested me, and there were many times when I wanted to give up. But we hadn't quit, and now those years of hard work were paying off. There's a Bible verse which says that those who sow in tears will reap in joy someday, and I really felt like that verse was coming to life at the ranch.

Some days, I'd daydream about what I'd left behind. I wondered, now that I was older and a bit wiser, what I might be able to do with a really talented horse, like the ones I used to train for George Zimmerman. But those days were long gone.

Or so I thought.

Despite the headaches of having old equipment, life was good at the ranch. Our numbers were up, and our finances were back on solid footing. I remember early on, we got a letter from a donor who'd offered to give us $100 a month, and we were nearly overcome with joy. In those days $100 meant we could keep the lights on and pay the phone bill.

But by 1987, things were looking up. Since it was the ranch's twenty-fifth anniversary, we decided to throw a party. We invited Dale and Opal to come back, and sent out invitations to donors and former campers alike. On the day of the anniversary celebration, the ranch grounds were packed with old friends. It felt like a giant family reunion.

In the audience that day was J. W. "Squat" Bailey and his wife, Betty. The Baileys were longtime friends of Melodie's parents, who'd come up for the anniversary from their home in Waynesboro, Georgia. The Baileys had a great reputation for raising Palomino horses on their farm and had been longtime supporters.

We wanted to thank them for their help, and honor them for their generous donations to the ministry in the past. It was because of faithful donors like the Baileys that our dreams for the ranch had been made possible.

We'd set up a little platform for the celebration, and I called Squat and Betty up to the microphone, planning on presenting them with a small token of our appreciation. But the Baileys had a surprise in store for me.

Before I could get a word out, Squat pulled out an envelope and handed it to me. Inside were the registration papers for a young stallion foal that had just been born on their farm in Georgia. They called him Paul's Little Red Berry, or Berry for short.

"All you have to do is drive down and get him," Squat said.

I was about to meet the horse who would change my life.

It's hard to put into words what I felt when I first saw Berry.

Before I came to the ranch, I thought training horses would be my life's work. I loved the excitement of competition, and the thrill of seeing thousands of hours of hard work paying off in the show ring, and dreamt of spending my life with great horses.

It wasn't only the prizes. I loved the competition itself, pushing myself and my horses through complicated maneuvers—racing through an arena at full speed and then making a hairpin turn through the slalom course, or coming to a sliding halt and then racing around in a circle, with the horse and rider working in perfect tandem. The joy of being lost in the moment, of having such perfect concentration that nothing else seemed to matter.

I love my horses, being with them and watching them play together. I love it, these days, when I climb into the saddle, without a rein in my hand or a bridle, and know that I can trust them completely. There's a great deal of joy and satisfaction. It's like being a kid all over again, without a care in the world, doing the one thing I love most.

When I became director of the ranch, I lost some of that joy. The work was hard but rewarding and important, and I don't regret my choices, not for one moment. But after a dozen years as an administrator of a nonprofit organization, sitting in an office most of the time, only squeezing in a few minutes to go out to the barn and spend time with my horses, I felt that I had lost something.

Whenever I was at the barn, I felt guilty, like I was wasting my time. Too many cares and worries had robbed me of some of the joy. Though I was proud of our accomplishments, and of how our staff had turned things around, I missed the horses.

Doing the Sermon on the Mount presentations helped. But even then I was always in a rush, hoping the truck wouldn't break down. And the horses were a means to an end, a way to get my point across, rather than true partners.

I'd come to believe that working at the ranch was my calling in life. And though I'd given up my dream of being a horse trainer, what I'd gained in my marriage to Melodie and my relationships with the staff, who'd become closer than family, was worth it. I had love, friends, and meaningful work, and for that I was grateful.

When the Baileys presented me with the papers for Berry, they did more than give me a horse. They gave me my dream back. It was like everything I'd given up was being paid back, with interest.

The weeks following the anniversary went by like a blur. For one thing, I had to make arrangements to go and get Berry. The Baileys lived about sixteen hours away, and bringing a new colt that distance was no simple matter. Seeing that I'd be taking him straight from his mother's side, I really needed to spend a little time with Berry, getting him ready to take such a trip.

And I needed to find the right equipment to bring him back with. I had the trailer I was using for Sermon on the Mount, and that was all right for a trip of a few hundred miles. But this was an 800-mile trip, one way.

Fortunately, some other friends of ours, Bill and Joan Wurst, had been at the anniversary as well, and when they heard about Berry they were delighted. They were taking a trip south anyway, and offered to drive me down to get Berry.

So that's how I found myself standing by a fence on the Baileys' farm, watching a young red Quarter Horse colt romping around his mother. He was beautiful even then, with a red coat so shiny that he literally glistened in the sun, a brilliant white blaze on his face.

Like any colt, he was a bit shy the first time I opened

the gate and walked into the pasture. But his natural curiosity outweighed any shyness he had, and before long he was standing beside me, nuzzling my hand, while I petted his mane and coat and wondered what I'd done to deserve such a gift of grace.

Berry would prove to be a very alert and responsive colt, and it wasn't long before he mastered some of the basics of being halter-broken and following a lead rope.

Like I said, I had given up on the idea that I would ever have the time to invest in training a horse again on a serious level. The camp took too much time, and there was only so much of me to go around. I felt guilty about spending time with the horses when so many other responsibilities—leading the staff, raising money, thinking about the ranch's future—needed my attention.

Accepting the Baileys' gift was much like becoming a parent. I would be responsible for guiding and shaping this young horse. In horse training, like parenting, there's no such thing as "quality time" only. Berry would need several hours of consistent attention and training every day for three or four years to get well established.

It wasn't a task I accepted lightly. It was, however, one I was looking forward to. Though I wouldn't have admitted it at the time, I was spending too much time cooped up in my office, and not enough time out in the barn. I had become, for lack of a better term, a real desk jockey. Getting outside and having daily, hands-on work with Berry was good for my soul.

Over those first two years, Berry's training went better than I could have hoped. A natural people-pleaser, he never gave me a bad day. Unlike Ribbon or some of the other horses I'd trained in the past, he never fought back or complained. Not that he was perfect, or got everything right the first time. But he was a delight to be around.

Before long, I had him out on the road with me for speaking engagements. Even as a colt, audiences would respond to him—people loved to watch him work. He was fast and strong and approached every task with a vigor and joy. He was having the time of his life, and so was I.

Those early days of Sermon on the Mount were a work in progress. Berry and I traveled thousands of miles together, during those early years, going wherever we were invited—schools and conferences and churches, sometimes in front of a few dozen people, other times drawing several hundred people.

Somewhere along the way, the truck would break down along the side of the road. Despite our best attempts to keep the equipment well maintained, some glitch would always come up, and we'd break down again. My team and I became experts at figuring out solutions for difficult situations.

Still, I was having a great time, and looked forward to years of partnership with Berry. Not long after he turned three, however, everything started to go south.

Things started to unravel when Berry and I began working on what's known as flying lead changes, a relatively advanced maneuver.

The idea is to get a horse to change directions while at a canter, which is a bit faster than a trot but not quite a gallop. When the horse goes to the right, their right front foot should look like it leads. When they go to the left, their left front foot should lead.

To master a flying lead change, the horse should switch easily from leading with their right to leading with their left, without slowing down or getting their feet tangled up. Instead, they should move smoothly from one to the other, like a dancer.

Until this point, Berry had mastered everything I'd tried to teach him. Now he struggled. His movements were clumsy and awkward, and no matter what I tried, he couldn't figure out the lead changes. One moment he'd be cantering beautifully, and the next he'd be stumbling and all out of sorts.

I'd never seen a horse respond in that way. He was working hard and willing to try, but the lead changes completely flummoxed him. It's not that Berry didn't want to do the lead changes; it's that he could not get the hang of them.

About this time, my friend John Lyons, the renowned horse trainer, was visiting the ranch. John was traveling the country and his business required an unexpected trip home to Colorado. Since he'd be gone for several weeks, he asked me to look after his horse, Bright Zip.

Zip is a legend among horse trainers. He and John traveled the country for years, giving exhibitions and horsemanship clinics. Later on in life, Zip went blind in both eyes, due to an adverse reaction to medication. Still he and John continued to work together. They were so in tune, and Zip so trusted John, that he could run at a gallop and turn on a dime without being able to see a thing.

When he came back from his trip to Colorado, I asked John to take a look at Berry. I explained the trouble we were having with flying lead changes, and John agreed to work with us for a few days. Even he was at a loss to understand why Berry had hit such a block, and couldn't help us find a way around it.

"I'm sorry, Lew," he said, "but I think you need to find another horse."

Not willing to give up, I called my old friend Ward Studebaker and asked him for advice. Ward offered to come and spend several days working with us. I was hopeful at first, but as the days wore on, that hope began to fade. When he left, he gave me the same advice that John had.

"Find another horse, Lew," Ward said, "He's not going to get it."

I hated to hear those words, because I trusted Ward. He always gave sound, wise advice, and never jumped to conclusions.

When Ward drove off, my heart sank, as if everything Berry and I had worked for was going right down the drain. I'd poured my life into this horse, and loved him, and now I was on the brink of losing all my hopes for him.

Something inside of me wasn't willing to give up. Perhaps it was pure stubbornness, but I felt that there was more I could learn from Berry. If we could overcome this roadblock, both of us would be better off.

Along with my stubbornness, I felt a sense of protectiveness toward Berry, much like a parent. After all this time together, I didn't want him to be defined by his limitations. If he failed in this challenge, it could set a pattern for the rest of his life, of giving up in the face of adversity.

To be honest, I had selfish reasons for not wanting to give up. I felt trapped and disappointed—I'd spent three years working with Berry, and he had such promise. I wasn't ready to walk away from him. Doing that would have left a bitter taste in my mouth for years, and I'd always wonder what might have been.

In the midst of this frustration, Berry taught me one of the most important lessons that a leader can ever learn. He taught me that in order to get past this obstacle, I needed to accept what we could not change, and embrace what we could change. It's not always easy to see the difference between the two.

With Berry, I needed to accept reality. The problem was this: he was not strong enough or flexible enough to master the flying lead changes. With that limitation, he would never master a flying lead change, no matter how many hours we practiced.

In an earlier chapter, we talked about what's called the 10,000 hour rule—to become an expert in any field requires 10,000 hours of practice. It's another version of the old saying that practice makes perfect. Except there is one caveat: you've got to practice the right things. Doing the wrong thing over and over again is pointless.

Since Berry had a physical limitation, I needed to accept that he was not ready to do a flying lead change. In order for him to succeed, we had to go back to the basics. I had to train him with exercises to become stronger and more flexible, until he had the capacity needed to master those maneuvers.

So we went backwards. We put our training on hold, and spent weeks on simple exercises, designed to build strength and flexibility in Berry. We worked on stretching techniques and new ways of warming him up, so when we finally attacked the lead changes again, he was more limber and agile. In the end, we transformed Berry from a willing but clumsy horse into a willing and athletic, capable horse.

Looking back at my time training Berry, I was reminded of a story I'd heard about the great racehorse, Seabiscuit. Though he eventually became one of the most celebrated thoroughbreds of the twentieth century, Seabiscuit's career had a rocky beginning. While he came from great bloodlines—his grandfather was the famed thoroughbred Man o' War—by the time he was two years old, Seabiscuit had lost seventeen races in a row. Things got so bad that his owner put him in a claiming race—the horsing world's equivalent of eBay.

Seabiscuit might have been lost in obscurity, had not a trainer named Tom Smith taken a liking to him. Smith convinced his boss, a man named Charles Howard, to take a chance on the horse. Howard, it seems, had a weakness for lost causes.

Smith teamed up Seabiscuit with a jockey named Red Pollard, and after a rocky start, the two clicked, and Seabiscuit started winning. And winning. And winning.

Eventually Seabiscuit would square off against War Admiral, who'd won the Triple Crown in 1937 and who was considered by many to be the greatest horse of his time.

That is, until November 1, 1938, when Seabiscuit beat War Admiral in a one-on-one match race at Pimlico racetrack outside of Baltimore. An estimated 40 million people listened to the radio broadcast of that race.

It was then, when Seabiscuit had his greatest triumph, that disaster struck. Not long afterward, he ruptured the suspensory ligament in his front left leg while preparing to run the Santa Anita Handicap, which was nicknamed the "hundred grander" for its $100,000 purse.

Smith and Howard feared he would never race again. A few months earlier, Seabiscuit's jockey, Red Pollard, had been nearly killed when a horse he was riding for a friend bolted. Pollard's leg was shattered and he was hospitalized for months. He was already blind in one eye, and his career seemed over as well.

But neither Pollard nor Seabiscuit were ready to give up. He and the horse convalesced together on Howard's farm. They walked for hours together, and little by little, rebuilt their injury-shattered bodies.

Despite their limitations, Seabiscuit and Pollard eventually began to race again. And on March 2, 1940, they won the Santa Anita, posting the fastest time in the history of that race, and ending Seabiscuit's career in a blaze of glory.

It would have been easy for Pollard and Seabiscuit to have given up, to have let their injuries and limitations define their lives. Likewise, it would have been easier for Smith to have overlooked a seventeen-time loser like Seabiscuit.

Berry and I have never won a race like the Santa Anita. Despite my great affection for him and my pride in his accomplishments, he's not Seabiscuit.

In his own way, Berry's story is almost as remarkable. After spending several months building his strength and flexibility, Berry and I tackled the flying lead changes again. This time, with his newfound athleticism, and his perseverance, he mastered them.

Over the next eight years, Berry and I would travel thousand of miles, giving presentations at small schools and churches tucked into the hollows of West Virginia and other Southern states, and later at larger events. Everywhere we went, Berry delighted the crowds who came to see him.

Flying lead changes were only the beginning for Berry. He eventually mastered even more difficult riding techniques. By the time he was six, I'd taught him how to ride without reins or bridle while blindfolded. With no means of seeing the way ahead of him, and without a rein to guide him, he learned to gallop and spin on a dime, and dozens of other intricate patterns, with only the slightest nudge or word from me to point the way.

There's a postscript to this story. When Berry was ten, he began to develop some problems breathing while galloping, which made doing Sermon on the Mount presentations harder for him. He didn't have the wind or endurance he'd once had. He'd also developed some soreness in his legs.

Worst of all, I began to suspect that he was going blind in one eye. That actually took me a while to discover, because he was so responsive to my instructions and we worked so closely together. In the end, he didn't need to see to know where he was going.

Berry and I took one last trip together, this time to a hospital, where veterinarians put him through a battery of tests. They confirmed my suspicions, that Berry was losing sight in one eye and that he had a chest condition that would permanently diminish his endurance. He'd be able to handle less strenuous workouts, but the Sermon on the Mount was too much for him. No amount of exercise or training could compensate for his condition.

After the examination, Berry's doctors showed me a pair of curious X-rays they'd taken. Berry, it turns out, had been born with some abnormal bone structure in his left rear hock and his right front hoof. Both of those areas are used when a horse makes a diagonal movement like a lead change.

Those bone abnormalities meant that movements like a lead change would be difficult for Berry. They wouldn't be painful, and there was no danger of permanent injury—instead he'd be naturally clumsy in those kinds of movements. They wouldn't hurt, but they'd be awkward.

If I'd seen those X-rays early on, I'd have thrown in the towel with Berry, and never seen the way through our struggles. I never would have seen what he could have become.

Not long after we returned home from the hospital, Berry retired from Sermon on the Mount. In the years that followed, he helped me train some of my students to overcome their weaknesses. Whenever a student would complain or say, "I can't do this," I introduced them to Berry.

And this one-eye-blind horse would show them the way.

Chapter 7

Fight or Flight

THE VOICE ON THE PHONE was desperate.

"You'd better get up here and get this horse," she said. "Get up here before my husband does, or he'll kill him."

The caller was a friend from a nearby farm, and her voice trembled as she spoke. For a year, I'd been giving her advice on how to deal with Winter, her Paint Stallion. Now something had gone wrong and it had scared the wits out of her.

"I'll be right there," I said.

Soon, I was pulling into the driveway of my friend's farm, towing a horse trailer behind the ranch's Ford pickup. As we walked out toward the horse barn, my friend relayed that afternoon's events.

For several years, my friend had been at a loss on how to deal with Winter, a stallion she'd raised. Winter was a beautiful horse, with a white coat with black spots on his backside. A strong and athletic horse, Winter had great potential, but had one drawback—a surly and aggressive attitude with women. Around a male rider or trainer he did all right, but with women, he become haughty and snotty, displaying an aggressive, macho attitude. He'd rear up on his hind legs and strike, refusing to comply with their instructions, and trying to intimidate them.

When she first came to see me, I gave my friend some pointers on how to establish firm boundaries with Winter and how to earn his respect as well as his trust. Winter was too clever for my friend, or any trainer, to simply manhandle. No one was going to force that horse to do anything he didn't want to do. He got his way by aggressiveness and intimidation, even around other horses.

Unless Winter could learn to control his impulses and to respect boundaries, he'd never progress in his training. He needed to learn how to rein in his aggression, before he or someone else got hurt or before my friend finally decided he was useless and had him put down.

As a last resort, I advised her to have him gelded— while that would ruin Winter as a stud horse by neutering him, it would cut off the testosterone that fueled his aggression. Better to have a sterile horse than an aggressive and unmanageable one.

When every other tactic had failed, my friend gave in and had Winter gelded. Even that didn't solve the problem completely. He was less aggressive, but never cooperative.

When I arrived at the farm, my friend was still trembling

from her encounter with him. She'd been mucking out Winter's stable and gotten careless just for a moment. She turned her back on him, and bent down to pick something up from the floor of the stable. In that split second he pounced on her, grabbing her with his teeth in the middle of her back and throwing her around the stable.

I'd known of other horses who'd turned on their owners like this, and it's never pretty, and sometimes fatal. Another friend of mine had bought a horse with similar tendencies at an auction several years earlier.

When she bought him, the horse seemed well trained and responsive. Once she got him home, though, he began to act out, pinning his ears back and swishing his tail in an agitated manner. At first, she thought he was out of sorts from being in a new environment, and thought he'd get over it soon enough and calm down.

Like Winter's owner, she turned her back on the horse, and in a split second he was after her. Instead of grabbing her in the middle of the back, this horse grabbed his owner by the neck and bit her savagely. Then he knocked her to the ground and began to stomp on her.

She escaped by playing dead, lying perfectly still despite the blows from the horse's hooves raining down on her. When the horse gave up and broke off the attack, he threw his head back and whinnied, as if gloating that he'd killed her.

By sheer luck, someone stopped by her home and

happened to walk into the barn. He saw my friend curled up on the ground and chased the horse away, before pulling her to safety. She was a terrible sight after the attack. That horse had gone psychotic and had to be destroyed.

Luckily for Winter's owner, Winter hadn't lost his mind. He wasn't bent on killing her; he only wanted to frighten and intimidate her.

My friend was saved by her choice of wardrobe. Working out in the barn, she was wearing a lightweight shirt with thin sleeves. As Winter tossed her around, the fabric tore. He lost his grip, and she went flying. She tumbled to the ground and rolled out of the stall, and was out of harm's way. She was shaken up, but not injured seriously.

She called me right afterwards and asked me to take him away. She didn't really care what I did with him—she wanted him gone before her husband got home and shot the horse right there and then.

I get calls about horses like Winter every once in a while, lost causes or reprobates, as we sometimes call them at the ranch, whose owners have lost all hope. On occasion, I've even worked with a horse that's killed someone, though it's usually been an accident, rather than a deliberate act.

Sometimes a horse is beyond help. If a horse is mentally ill, unstable, or dangerous, I won't work with it. But Winter wasn't psychotic—he was a bully that had finally gone too far. He needed a sharp lesson in reality. And he needed someone to show him a better way than aggression and intimidation to get what he wanted out of life.

One of the keys to being a good trainer—or any kind of leader—is to focus on needs, not behavior. Oftentimes we get so focused on someone's negative behavior that we don't stop to evaluate what is causing the person to act or to react in that manner.

I'm not talking about some touchy-feely, why-can't-we-all-get-along approach. Winter had deliberately harmed his trainer, and that was unacceptable. The easy solution would have been to put him down, to say that he wasn't worth saving. But Winter wasn't at that point yet.

What I had to figure out was, why had he attacked my friend? What had gone wrong in his life to cause such a reaction? Why was this horse filled with such anger?

His behavior was only a symptom. I needed to figure out what was causing the behavior.

One cause became clear after I'd talked with Winter's owner. Because he was in training, she'd been giving him a high-powered horse feed. That feed gave him plenty of energy, but he wasn't working enough of that energy off and it kept him going at a frantic pace, as if he'd been on a steady diet of Red Bull or some other high-caffeine, high-sugar energy drink. Taking him off the high-powered feed would help Winter clear his head, and allow him to think straight.

When he arrived at the ranch, I put Winter out to pasture

with a group of older geldings, and let them go to work on him. Horses are herd animals by nature, with a pecking order that puts every horse in its place. Winter had been ruling the roost at his owner's farm, and had gotten a big head.

These older geldings weren't going to be impressed by a young punk with an over-inflated ego. In a few weeks, they'd reminded him that he was a horse, and not a particularly special one at that.

In his book, *A Horse and His Boy*, C. S. Lewis writes about a proud warhorse named Bree, who spends most of his time boasting about how brave and accomplished he is. The boy in the story is a poor fisherman's son named Shasta, who turns out to be more than meets the eye. At a crisis point in the story Bree and Shasta, along with their traveling companions—a girl named Aravis and her mare Hwin—are attacked by a lion. Bree flees for his life in a panic, while Shasta faces the lion, and fights him off.

Afterward, Bree is ashamed and humbled by his behavior, and realizes that he's not quite the brave warhorse he believed he was. With that perspective, Bree becomes a better and happier horse.

Winter was a bit like Bree, too full of himself for his own good. The geldings made a start of bringing him back to reality. They also took the edge off Winter's anger.

When I work with a horse, one of my main training tools is pressure. Since horses can't talk—aside from in C. S. Lewis's

Narnia books—they rely on the nonverbal communication of body language and pressure to communicate. I use pressure—with a rope, or by waving a flag, or by getting close to a horse, to get my message across.

With an angry horse, like an angry person, pressure is counterproductive. There was too much noise from the emotions inside Winter, and he could not hear me. I needed to ratchet Winter's emotions down so he was able to listen and respond. Once Winter had gotten back to some semblance of a normal life, and wasn't seething with anger, I began working with him.

I set up a round pen where there were enough boundaries to keep him honest, and got after him. At first, he acted all haughty and snotty, but that died down when he realized it wasn't doing him any good. Instead of reacting to his behavior, I put steady pressure on him, asking him to comply without complaining. Every time he did, he got a reward of released pressure.

Eventually, Winter began to see that by cooperating with a trainer, his life would get better. That gave him a sense of hope, and he began to progress. Since he'd had such a hard time with women riders, I asked some of our women staff to ride him—once he'd calm down—and rewarded his good behavior.

At the end of my retraining, Winter was a different horse. Once a menace who delighted in temper tantrums, he became one of the most beloved horses on the ranch.

In the end, Winter's problem wasn't so much his behavior. His problem was an attitude of disrespect. Without clear boundaries and consistent authority, he became insecure and took control.

Without hope, without a sense that life can get better, horses—like people—can easily fall into a sense of despair. Winter had no reason to believe that cooperating with his trainer would make his life better. Without hope, he had no incentive to change.

To fix Winter, I didn't need to change his behavior. I needed to change his beliefs—to get him to put his faith in me, and not in his own aggressive control.

Winter had learned that by being aggressive and using intimidation, he could get what he wanted. For a while it worked. He was well fed, had a comfortable stable, and had his trainer doing things his way, not her way.

That eventually fell apart, when he pushed things too far. Once that happened, Winter had no clue about how to put his life back together.

When I train a horse, it's a constant balancing act. If the training is too easy, a horse will lose interest and become bored and sloppy. If the training is too hard, and I ask too much, my horse will either lose hope or become defiant.

When a challenge or training problem is too big, a horse can get overwhelmed and react in anger. In those cases, the first response is fight or flight. The horse either runs away and tries to ignore the problem, or they put up a stink and refuse to comply with the trainer's request, in hopes that the trainer will give up, believing the training is too much of a hassle.

Sound familiar? Anyone who's been a parent has seen these responses. If we're honest, we might admit that we have tried the fight or flight response with a boss or a parent or a spouse. If things go on too long, fight or flight can turn into anger and despair, and a sense of hopelessness for people, or for horses.

When I first met the Smiths, they knew something about hopelessness.

They were both surgeons, who'd passed up prestigious big-city residencies to practice in small-town Pennsylvania, in hope of finding a good quality of life for their family.

For years things went well for the Smiths. They were blessed with four beautiful and talented children, and built up successful medical practices. They had everything going for them.

But as time went by, the pressures of running those practices and maintaining a busy family life took a toll on their marriage. Over the years small hurts and misunderstandings got glossed over, and the pressures of life began to crack their relationship.

Finally it broke. By the time I met Dr. Beth, they'd been separated for several years, and things looked hopeless.

I didn't learn all this the first time I met Dr. Beth. In fact it took quite a while before she told me much about her story. If I'd pried into her background at the beginning, things would probably not have turned out well at all.

We met Dr. Beth through my mother. In her later years, my mother had come to live with us at the ranch, and she'd developed some stomach problems. Dr. Beth was treating her, and one day my mother introduced me to Dr. Beth while I was visiting her at the hospital.

My mother was always interested in people, and it wasn't too long before she'd befriended Dr. Beth. At that time she was raising the four kids on her own, and was about at her wits' end, especially in dealing with her teenaged boys.

Mother invited her out to the ranch to see a Sermon on the Mount presentation, and to her surprise, Dr. Beth agreed. She and the kids came out to the ranch, and something about the presentation resonated with them. Before long, they were regular visitors, and Dr. Beth's son Ben would eventually come and spend the summer with us at the camp.

Once we'd become friends and she trusted us, Dr. Beth told us the story of her marriage, and of the unresolved conflict. At this point, they'd been separated for nine years, with no resolution in sight. But they'd experienced enough pain and hurt to know things couldn't continue on the same path.

There's a preacher named Ed Stetzer who likes to say that people won't change until the pain of remaining the same becomes overwhelming. That's a bit how the Smiths felt. Anything had to be better than their present reality.

So Dr. Beth asked Melodie and me if there was any chance her marriage could be saved. I didn't know at the time but we offered to meet with them, to find out if there was any hope left for them. Before we knew it, they had come in for counseling.

Melodie and I do a lot of marital counseling. We've both earned degrees in that area—as well as having learned from the ups and downs of our own marriage—and have built up a reputation for helping people.

By the time married couples get to us, they are usually at the end of their rope. They have read the books, seen the videos, gone to the conferences, and none of it has worked.

It's only the desperate people who come to us—they have exhausted all their options. The rumor is that we are straightforward and don't sugar-coat things. We don't fix marriages but we can help people who are ready to change.

The first time we met, you could cut the tension in the air with a knife. They sat at opposite ends of the couch, scarcely willing to look at each other. They were sensitive, afraid, and ready to bolt. It seemed there was little hope of recovery.

Like many people stuck in difficult circumstances, they'd come to believe that the only way things would get better was if the other person changed. It's like that at work—if only my boss were more understanding, or I had better co-workers, things would be different. It's like that at church—if only the preacher weren't so boring, my life would be better. And it's like that in marriage. If only my spouse would understand me, I could be happy.

Nobody ever changes unless they see some evidence of hope. Something to put their trust in—something that allows them to set down their defenses and try something new.

People who have lost hope need a stable point of reference, something to put their faith in. They need to put their faith in something or someone who is trustworthy.

In those counseling sessions, the Smiths found enough hope to start over. It wasn't easy. There was a lot of anger, disappointment, rejection, and loneliness to work through. But they created a safe place in that counseling that gave them hope that their relationship could be healed. Over several months they rebuilt their marriage and renewed their vows, putting their family back together.

The kids didn't believe them at first, and put the Smiths through the wringer, testing them to make sure this renewed marriage would last. In recent years, their boys have gotten married themselves, and they've put the lessons their parents learned to good use.

A marriage that was brittle and could have easily ended was saved.

When I first met Rowdy, I knew I was in for it.

Rowdy was a middle-aged gelding, who was full of himself, and who wasn't going to let anyone tell him what to do. So much so, that when his owner brought him into the corral, she led him with a chain, not a rope. That chain, and the cue stick in her hand, were the only things that kept him in line.

When I do a Sermon on the Mount presentation, I often ask for a horse who has had trouble getting along with a rider or trainer, and Rowdy fitted that profile to a tee. Rowdy was no dummy. He knew that he was stronger than any trainer, and understood that if he reared up on his hind legs, he had the advantage over his handler.

He also knew about the power of his head. Earlier, we talked about how, when I was young, I misunderstood horses. I believed that the key to controlling a horse was to control their head, by yanking on their reins or lead rope. But a horse's true power comes from his hips, not his head.

Rowdy knew that, and so he kept the focus on his head. So he'd pull back on the reins or lead rope, or bear his teeth and face the trainer. The trainer could easily get sucked into a power struggle with Rowdy, and never get anywhere with him. It's like a pair of kids stuck in a game of one upmanship. A complete waste of time.

My response was to focus on his hips, not his face. I gave Rowdy a length of rope, and asked him to move. I gave him enough space that he didn't feel crowded, but not so much that he could run away. All the while I watched his response.

If Rowdy was ignoring me, and trying to provoke a fight, he'd yank on the rope and pull it tight. I didn't yank back but I kept a steady pressure on. When he yielded a bit, and eased on the rope, so would I. That release of pressure acted like a reward for Rowdy. If he gave in, he got what he wanted.

A horse like Rowdy needs hope. He needed an incentive or reward for cooperating. I'm not talking about a bribe to earn a horse's cooperation. Instead, he needs an incentive or reward for doing the right thing first.

In other words, I had to be smarter than the horse.

I call this kind of tactic the soft answer to anger. Not a weak answer, giving in to Rowdy's demands. But a soft answer, that defused and redirected his anger and attention. I wanted to make him think and choose a different response.

There's a great story told about Jesus in the New Testament. In his day, Israel was occupied by the Roman Empire, and for most of the population, Rome was seen as the enemy.

The Romans made all the rules, enforced the law with brutal violence, and made the people pay heavy taxes. They were extremely unpopular, especially with the religious leaders, who prayed that God would send someone to rescue them.

Jesus also ran afoul of the religious leaders of his day, because he challenged their authority. Understandably, this made them angry and so some leaders conspired to find ways to get rid of him.

At one point, someone asked Jesus a question about paying taxes to Rome. It was a loaded question. If Jesus said yes, they should pay taxes to Rome, he'd look like a Roman sympathizer and that would turn people against him. If he said no they shouldn't, then Jesus would be a rabble-rouser and in trouble with the law. People who didn't pay taxes to Rome didn't live long.

Instead, Jesus asked a question. "Show me the coin used to pay taxes," he said.

His questioners fished out a coin, which had a portrait of Caesar, the Roman emperor, engraved on it.

"Whose portrait is this?" Jesus asked.

"Caesar's," someone replied.

"Give to Caesar what is Caesar's, and to God what is God's," Jesus said.

That's a perfect soft answer. Rather than taking sides in a debate on taxes, he turned the question back on his opponents. They had to figure out how to respond next.

There's another soft answer in the Bible, found in the Old Testament. Most of us are familiar with the story of David and Bathsheba. David, who was the king, saw Bathsheba, a beautiful woman, bathing naked on her rooftop. She was married but her husband was always away fighting for the king.

David wanted her, and so being king, summoned

Bathsheba to his bedroom, and we all can guess what happened next.

A few months later, though, Bathsheba sent word that she was pregnant. Since her husband had been away, the pregnancy was proof that she and the king had been having an affair.

David summoned her husband back from the war, hoping that he'd sleep with Bathsheba—so that when he discovered she was pregnant, her husband would think the child was his. But her husband, an honorable man, refused to sleep with his wife while his men were out in the field, fighting for the king.

Desperate to cover up the affair, David ordered Bathsheba's husband back to the war. He told another officer to put him at the front line, and then to fall back, abandoning him to the enemy. He was killed, and after a brief period of mourning, Bathsheba married King David.

Now news of something like this never stays hidden. Everyone knew what the king had done, and were appalled by it. No one wanted to confront David to his face—at least no one who valued his head.

But a prophet named Nathan had a better idea. He came to David with a tale of woe. A terrible injustice had taken place in the kingdom, Nathan said.

In a certain village lived a poor man and a rich man. The rich man had much property and many sheep, and was wealthy beyond compare. The poor man had very little. His

142

prized possession was one sheep, whom he kept as a pet for his children.

But one night the rich man had a guest. And instead of slaughtering one of his own sheep and feeding it to the guest, he stole the poor man's pet, killed it, and had it roasted as dinner for his guest.

David, as you can imagine, was livid and vowed to punish the rich man. "Who is this man?" he asked.

Bingo!

Nathan said, "You are."

In that soft answer, David realized that Nathan knew about Bathsheba. He also realized the horror of what he'd done.

David did all the work. He changed and tried to make amends for his crime, not because Nathan angrily confronted him, but because he was ashamed on the inside of what he'd done.

Not long ago, I was asked to travel to Utah, to give a Sermon on the Mount presentation in a small desert town. Some Baptists had invited me in, hoping to foster peace in their town. Typical of Utah, most of the people who lived in the town were Mormons. But some Baptists had also settled there, and the two groups were at odds.

No one remembered who had started the conflict, but there were plenty of hard feelings to go around. The two groups lived separate lives. They lived apart, socialized apart, and shunned each other's company. Neither group trusted the other.

As you can guess, this made life pretty miserable. The one thing the Baptists and the Mormons shared in common was a love for horses. So the Baptists invited me in the hope that I could break the ice between the two groups.

It was rough going. A large crowd had gathered but they were segregated, with the Baptists on one side and the Mormons on the other. I began to work with a mustang who had been run in right off the desert.

He was a strong and healthy colt, who'd never spent any time with people. His mane and tail were knotted and twisted, and he had some bite marks on him from tussling with other horses. We spent several hours together.

As I worked, I noticed one man on the Mormon side come down from the crowd and stand by the fence. We started talking as I worked, and it was clear he knew his way around horses.

Getting a wild mustang settled down takes a while. Usually I can calm a horse down pretty quickly so I can put a bridle on it, but in this case, I needed to take a different approach. I asked the man who'd been observing me to lend a hand.

I'm a terrible roper. I've worked with horses for years, and it's one of the skills that has always eluded me. I can usually rope a horse that's been running around, but not until the horse, and anyone watching, has had a good laugh.

This time, I asked my observer if he'd mind roping the horse. "Sure," he said, and made his way over to the gate of the round pen. Within a few minutes, he had the horse lassoed and handed the rope over to me.

As the program went along, I talked to the audience about the inner battle this mustang was facing. He could keep running and wear himself out. Or he could give in a bit, and trust me.

At some point in the program, I noticed that the man who was watching me had begun to cry.

Eventually the mustang gave in enough to let me get close, and after an hour and a half, he let me put a saddle on him and ride. It was quite a transformation for this wild mustang.

After I was done, the man who'd been watching me came up and we talked. For most of his life, he'd been estranged from his family, and it made him miserable and angry. Watching that mustang had been like seeing himself in the mirror. And he didn't like what he saw and wanted to change.

That conversation and my visit to the town didn't change that community overnight. But it did break open a little space for hope for that man, and for the audience.

Afterward I could see a few of the Baptists and Mormons talking to one another, if not in friendly tones, at least in civil ones. For one night, they didn't see each other as enemies.

If I'd come in and given a leadership seminar about how we all have to get along, and about diversity and about respecting different people's viewpoints, the audience would have applauded nicely and gone home. They might not even have shown up in the first place.

But I gave them a soft answer instead. I made some space for them to set aside their anger and hostility, and to think about what they had in common. That's a start. There was room for more movement in the right direction.

CHAPTER 8

READY FOR A CRISIS

THEY CALLED IT THE MIRACLE on the Hudson.

At about 3:30 in the afternoon on January 15, 2009, US Airways Flight 1549 took off from runaway number 4 at LaGuardia Airport in New York, with 155 passengers on board, headed for Charlotte, on the first leg of a cross-country journey. It was a clear, cold, New York afternoon—a perfect day for flying.

Not long after take-off, however, something went drastically wrong. As the plane banked over the Hudson River, it encountered a flock of Canadian geese. Though those geese weigh less than ten pounds, they can wreak havoc with a plane's engines. Several were sucked into the engines, causing both to go out, sending the aircraft plummeting toward the icy Hudson.

Like all flight crews, the pilots and flight attendants aboard Flight 1549 had trained for emergency landing and before this flight, the flight attendants had instructed their passengers what to do "in the unlikely event of a water landing." Most of those passengers, especially the experienced ones, had likely tuned out the familiar words.

Now that unlikely event was a reality.

By all accounts, the crew acted heroically, putting their years of training into practice. The pilot, Chesley B. "Sully" Sullenberger III, kept the plane level as it crashed into the river. Despite the understandable panic among the passengers, the flight attendants kept their heads. When a group of passengers rushed to the rear of the plane, hoping to get out the back door, the captain and crew convinced them to stop before their added weight forced the tail to sink. While some passengers grabbed for their luggage or struggled from their seats, the flight attendants kept them calm and orderly, getting everyone out of the plane and on the wings.

It must have been a terrifying experience, standing on those wings in twenty-degree temperatures, a few inches above the frigid waters of the Hudson. Anyone who fell in the water would likely die of hypothermia in minutes. There was no hope of swimming to shore. Some passengers had to wade out into knee-deep water to reach the edge of the wings, in order to make space for everyone to get off the plane. And all the while the passengers knew that the plane could go down at any minute.

A few of them were old enough to remember the last time something like this had happened. Back in 1982, an Air

Florida 737 plunged into the Potomac River in Washington, D.C., in the middle of winter. Of the eighty-three people on board, only five survived.

This time, the outcome was happier. Thanks to the fast action of the crew and some local ferry-boat captains, along with rescue crews, everyone was saved. In fact, by the time the news of the crash reached the airwaves, the crisis was over, and all the passengers were ashore, and being treated by paramedics. No wonder people across the country called it a miracle.

I don't know what part divine intervention played on that frozen January afternoon, but one thing I can say for sure: Things would have turned out much differently if the crew hadn't been prepared for a crisis. Without the right training and preparation, they would have failed their greatest test.

Thankfully, most of us will never have to face a crisis of this magnitude. But all of us will face tests of some kind. And our success or failure will largely depend on the kinds of habits, skills, and character we've developed ahead of time.

When I work with a horse, I have one ultimate goal in mind—to develop them into a dependable and trustworthy horse. No matter how talented they are physically, if I can't trust a horse, then they are of no use.

Dr. Martin Luther King Jr. once dreamed that his children would be judged by "the content of their character," not the color of their skin or any external factor.

That's what I am after. It's easy to judge a horse by

external factors but I want to build up the content of their character. We do that in steps.

The first step, as we talked about earlier, is to change the horse's beliefs. Most horses, like most people, are naturally independent and self-sufficient. They look out for number one, as the old saying goes.

As we've seen, that selfishness limits a horse's—or a person's—potential. If a horse, like my mare Ribbon, refuses to cooperate and to work hard, they'll never reach their full potential. They'll never overcome the obstacles they face in life.

On the other hand, even a horse with limitations—like Berry or even Peyote—can overcome those limits. It starts by changing their beliefs, teaching them to focus on the trainer and not on their own needs or limitations.

The second step is making choices. My horses choose every day whether to partner with me and give their all, or to remain inwardly focused.

There's a parallel here to the human world. The crew of Flight 1549 chose to be trained in how to respond in an emergency. Some of the training was likely boring and tedious, with constant repetition until they got it right. It was likely hard work, and I'm sure sometimes they wondered what the point was. They must have gotten tired of reading out those emergency instructions, knowing that many of the passengers weren't listening anyway.

With repetition, choices become habits. I reward my

horses every time they make the right choice, and over time, those choices build good habits of listening and perseverance.

Those habits build character, in the same way that constant training helps a runner build the endurance needed to run a marathon. There are no shortcuts to training for a marathon. You can't prepare your body to run more than twenty-six miles without stopping in a few days or weeks. It takes months of running, day in and day out, to build the muscle strength and endurance a marathon requires.

In the same way, it took Berry months of exercise and stretching to build the strength and flexibility he needed to do flying lead changes and overcome his physical limitations.

The problem with a crisis or a test is this—we never know when it is coming.

For my Quarter Horse Stallion Spark, one of his first tests arrived the day he met the Tennessee Walking Horse.

We were doing a Sermon on the Mount presentation, and Spark was helping me saddle-break a three-year-old horse who'd never been ridden before.

Mostly, when I'm doing presentation, I work one on one with the horse in a sixty-foot-wide round pen. But there's another way to go about this. On the day we met the Tennessee Walking Horse, Spark was assisting me, acting as a mentor or guide for the younger horse.

We call this approach "ponying," and it's helpful on two levels. First, the older horse often has a calming effect on a young, unbroken horse, especially if that horse hasn't spent much time around people. The older horse acts as a mentor, a reassuring presence to build the younger horse's confidence. Since horses have a pecking order, the young horse will often defer to the older horse, and be more willing to pay attention.

Second, the younger horse can mimic the behavior and attitude of the older horse and so can learn by example. That's the message I wanted to get across in this session—to show how the values and character traits Spark had learned could be passed on to a younger, less experienced colt.

Spark and I had come a long way since the first day we met, when he was a little less than a year old. He'd been raised on the Crow Creek division of the C.S. Ranch in New Mexico by my friends Warren and Mary Davis, and I'd driven out west to pick him up.

The ranch utilizes over 300,000 acres in a beautiful mountain setting, with nothing but wide open spaces for miles around. Bordered by the Sangre de Cristo mountains, it boasts some of the most beautiful sunsets in the nation. Spark had spent most of his first year wandering those open ranges with minimal human contact, and was relatively independent.

He is excitable by nature—so much so that the first time I took off his halter, he reacted by jumping up against me and stomping his front legs, cracking three of my ribs. For a stallion, he's sensitive as well. He doesn't like to be hit or crowded by another horse or touched on his nose. As a young colt, he reacted whenever I brought a lead rope near him. To Spark, it looked like a snake on the ground, and he'd like nothing better than to stomp it.

He was particular irritated by sounds, like the snap of a rein being slapped against the side of a horse, or the sound of hoofs walking across a metal surface. So I had to a lot of work to do with Spark in the early days.

He's calmed down significantly, and has become an expert at ignoring outside distractions and being completely focused on listening to my directions, even when that means ignoring the things that would otherwise irritate him. Spark is so responsive to my commands, that I'll often ride him bridleless, using nothing but the pressure of my legs or a spoken word to guide him. His focus makes him well suited for ponying. Oftentimes I'll ride him with another horse's lead rope dallied to the horn of my saddle.

The Tennessee Walking Horse colt seemed like a good candidate for ponying. Like many young horses I work with, the colt had been well fed and cared for but his training had been neglected. As far as I knew, he didn't have any behavior problems, aside from being a bit spoiled.

Still, Walking Horses are known for being even-tempered and easygoing, and while the colt was barely halter broken, he seemed agreeable enough. Until I grabbed hold of his lead rope.

The second I dallied the rope around the saddle horn, the Walking Horse began showing his true colors. He leaned over and snapped at Spark, trying to sink his teeth into my horse's side, and then kicked at Spark.

As a stallion, Spark's natural reaction was to retaliate. But that's not how I had trained him, and so despite the abuse of this spoiled brat of a colt, Spark stood his ground.

I asked Spark to move forward, hoping to put a little distance between him and the colt, while at the same time distracting the colt from lashing out at Spark.

As soon as Spark moved, the colt bolted. Before I knew it, the two horses were at full gallop, barreling around the rodeo arena. Like most arenas, it had a wide dirt floor surrounded by a steel fence that separated the performing area from the bleachers where the spectators sat. A gasp rose up from the crowds as they realized I was stuck on the back of one of the two runaway horses with no bridle to guide Spark back under control.

By this point, I could tell Spark was ticked. If he'd wanted to retaliate against the colt, I wouldn't have blamed him. As the two horses raced around the arena, it would have been easy for him to ignore me and to focus on his new found rival.

Despite his irritation and the excitement of the chase, Spark never lost his head. He knew that no matter what was going on around him, he could look to me for guidance. As we galloped, I cued him to turn, directing him towards one of the steel fences.

As he approached the wall, Spark did what I had trained him to do—he dug in his back feet and slid us to a stop. Seeing the fence in front of him, the colt did the same.

Whew, I thought. *That was a close one.*

As soon as we turned away from the fence, the colt bolted again, and once more we were off on a merry chase. When I turned Spark toward the fence, the colt, who was still dallied to us, showed no sign of stopping. *This is going to hurt,* I thought.

Looking back, it seems funny now—the thought of racing around that arena with the two horses, with no reins to guide Spark. More than anything, it reminds me of a scene from an old movie, where the driver and passenger of a car are arguing about which turn to take, and both grab onto the wheel as the car races down the highway. As they both yank on the steering wheel, it comes loose, and now the car is out of control, with no way to steer.

There was real danger in that moment. Crashing into a steel-pipe fence while attached to 2,000 pounds of horseflesh would have been ugly. Several years ago, I saw a young colt who'd gotten so excited that he tried to leap a fence and ended up impaled on one of the posts. He survived, but was permanently impaired because of the torn muscles in his chest.

And I've known of riders who've been seriously injured after being thrown from a horse. Ralph, who is my right-hand man at the ranch, fell from a horse back in 2008, and suffered such a severe concussion that we feared he had irreparable brain damage. For months, he couldn't concentrate and would forget where he was.

Once, while at a church service, he got so confused that he sat down next to a woman in one of the pews, thinking he was sitting next to his wife. Then he looked up and realized he didn't know who she was. "You're not my wife, are you?" he said, with a sheepish grin on his face. Ralph did eventually make a full recovery, but he had us worried for a while.

As we approached the fence for a second go round, time seemed to slow down, like the pause just before a train wreck, when you can see it coming but are helpless to stop it. For a fleeting moment, I thought, *This horse is not going to stop.*

Just shy of the fence, Spark put on the brakes and he and the colt skidded to a halt once more.

By this time, the colt had run out of steam. While he wasn't quite ready to give me his full attention, he wasn't about to bolt again. Within about half an hour, he'd begun to listen, and allowed me to saddle and ride him, leaving us with a relatively happy ending. All's well that ends well, as Shakespeare said.

If Spark had been a different horse and hadn't been able to hear my voice when that colt bolted, it would have been a different story. Like the crew of Flight 1549, Spark and I started our training long before we ever faced a crisis.

As I mentioned, he was pretty wound up and excitable as a young colt. Once I had got him to stop wanting to stomp on his lead rope as if it were a snake, we went to work in earnest. My first goal was to grab Spark's attention, so that no matter what was going on around him, he'd always look to me, and focus on my directions, not on his circumstances.

When dealing with a horse that's excitable or easily distracted, the natural reaction is to try to desensitize him. That's an approach police departments often use while training their mounted patrols. Because of the nature of their work, police horses are often in loud, dangerous situations. One of their most common responsibilities is crowd control, which is uncomfortable for horses. They don't like crowds of people, or the sound of yelling or sirens, and strange people touching their faces or manes and tails. All of that can happen in a crowd.

To compensate for this, police horses are often trained to ignore any distractions around them. If a horse gets used to a siren going off around him, then he won't panic when a police car pulls up, with its siren wailing. Likewise, if the horse is taught to ignore groups of strangers, then he's less likely to react when he is stuck in the middle of a crowd.

The downside to all this is the horses can become so desensitized that they even ignore the officers riding on their backs. In a crowd of people, or a crisis situation, it can be a recipe for disaster.

That's what the St. Paul, Minnesota police department was worried about in the summer of 2007. The following year, the city would be hosting the Republican National Convention. Along with the delegates, this was likely to attract thousands of protesters, some of them very angry about the direction in which the country was going.

Angry protesters and horses don't mix very well. The department had heard horror stories about protesters throwing broken glass on the sidewalk in front of horses, hoping to cut their feet; or protesters yanking on the reins of horses or crowding around them, trying to spook them.

The last thing the department wanted was for that to happen and for one of their horses to overreact, resulting in injury. So they asked me to come in and work with some of their mounted patrol officers.

The officers were great to work with—highly dedicated and eager to improve their skills. To be honest, however, their training had been inconsistent. Most were riding their own horses, so there were a variety of breeds in the patrol, with varied skill levels. Some officers were highly trained, others were not.

One horse in particular caught my eye. A huge Draft Horse I nicknamed "Dozer," as in bulldozer, because of his massive size—he was well over 2,000 pounds. Dozer was a perfect example of a desensitized horse.

He had an easy nature and nothing seemed to faze him—including his rider. That made Dozer the department's greatest asset for crowd control, and its biggest liability. Standing 16 to 17 hands high and backed by 2,000 pounds of muscle, Dozer could bust up any crowd. Unfortunately, once he got started, there was no stopping him. He'd learned his lessons too well.

So I put Dozer through some training exercises and began to focus him on learning to listen. In some ways, it was like giving a set of hearing aids to someone who'd gone deaf. Then I had the officers from the patrol work their horses, in the same way, so that when something startled them or made them feel uncomfortable, they'd tune out everything but their rider's voice and directions.

I also told them about my own experiences with Spark. When Spark was two, he and I took a trip to Ohio, where I was scheduled to do a Sermon on the Mount presentation. It was a relatively short trip so I didn't have all my equipment with me, and the church that was hosting us wasn't able to come up with a round pen for me to use.

So we improvised. The church set up seating on the front lawn, which faced a state highway. I parked my rig and trailer on the church's lawn, between the building and the highway, so we'd at least have a barrier between where I was working and the road.

On one side was the audience; on the other was my

trailer, with Spark and myself between them. There were no side barriers, but I wasn't too concerned. We weren't going to be racing around the lawn too much, so I felt we were relatively safe.

After showing the audience some basic tricks that Spark had learned, I got to the main event. The focus that night was on trust, and how to have inner confidence and peace, no matter what our circumstances. To demonstrate that principle, I'd set up an obstacle course on the lawn. Spark and I had been working on similar courses back home at the ranch.

Because they are prey animals, horses are cautious by nature. When they are running on familiar surfaces—grass, dirt, gravel—horses run comfortably, without any concerns. When they see something unusual, say a tarp or a board or something else out of the ordinary, they hesitate and prepare to run from it.

So I set up a load of debris on the lawn, with some of my gear and a few items borrowed from the church. I started with some crates and a ladder, followed by a saddle rack from the truck, and covered it all with a blue tarp. In between the debris I made a narrow path for Spark to make his way through.

I stood on one side, in front of the audience, and Spark stood by the trailer. Then I called him to me.

When he heard me, he looked up and started walking forward. As he approached the debris, he paused and reached out one of his feet to test and see where it was safe for him to walk. All the while I called to him, and so despite his uncertainty about the debris, he started walking towards me.

Part way through, Spark took a misstep. I'd laid the tarp over the saddle rack, and on that rack there was one small gap, just wide enough for a horse's foot to get through. We'd been working with racks and tarps and other obstacles for months, and Spark never had a problem.

This time, however, he put his foot in precisely the wrong spot, and it slipped through the rungs at the bottom of the saddle rack. When he pulled his foot back, the whole pile collapsed, trapping his leg in the debris.

Suddenly, I was scared. Here was a three-year-old colt, reactionary by nature, with his leg trapped in a pile of debris and a tarp fluttering right in his face. Worse yet, I wasn't anywhere near him, so I couldn't hold him in place long enough to get his leg clear. And there was no perimeter fence to protect him from running off or dragging the debris madly through the audience. Every instinct in Spark's body was telling him to bolt, which was the absolute worst thing he could have done.

As Spark began to lift his foot and try to tug it clear, I called out to him. "Spark," I said. "Stay."

Though he was only three years old, Spark knew that he could trust me. So despite the rising panic in his chest, he held his foot still. Calmly I walked over to him, and asked for a few volunteers. Three men from the audience stood up and within a few minutes, they'd cleared the debris and Spark was free.

The audience, most of whom had no idea how bad things could have gotten, broke out in applause. But Spark didn't panic, and because he trusted me, we were able to cope with the crisis and come through unscathed.

I don't know about you, but there have been many times in my life when I've felt trapped, like Spark did, and all I wanted to do was run away. Even though I knew it was the wrong thing to do in the long run, the temptation to flee in hard times is almost overwhelming.

As I write these words, our country is going through a difficult time. People have lost their jobs or their retirement savings and wonder how they are going to make ends meet in the future. Those who haven't lost their jobs wonder if they'll be next. At times like this, it's easy to get overwhelmed by fear and uncertainty.

Like Spark, we need to find something or someone to hold onto in days like these. For me, it's my faith, the belief that God is with me even in the hardest time.

That doesn't mean that life is easy or without pain. But even in the most difficult times, I know I'm not alone. That faith, that assurance, helps me to keep walking even when I can't see the way ahead.

That moment on the lawn in Ohio became a turning point for Spark and me. He knew he could trust me to keep him safe, and I knew that I had his full attention. We've become true partners in the months and years that have followed.

We've become so in tune that when we are out on a ride, I have been known to ride him bridleless, with a coffee cup in one hand and my laptop in the other, while I'm searching for a wi-fi Internet signal.

Not long ago, we were in Joshua, Texas, to give a presentation at a cowboy church. The church has invited me to speak to them several times, and every visit, it seems the church is bigger. The first time I went to this church, there were only thirty or so people, and I set up my round pen right in the middle of the congregation.

The next time I came back, there were 400 people there. The time after that, there were 1,200 and they'd moved to a larger building—a barn-style building with a dirt floor and folding chairs all around.

Each time I spoke, because the crowds were bigger, my round pen started getting smaller. Before too long, it seemed like the horse and I were right on top of each other, which made both of us nervous. The horse felt crowded and wanted to bolt over the fence.

Finally I told the church that though I loved to come and speak to them, this setup wasn't working. So the next time they invited me, the church rented an indoor arena that seated 2,500 for the weekend.

I'd been assured by the church that this setting would be perfect, with plenty of room for my sixty-foot-wide round pen. Because there were bleachers in the arena, the congregation would get a better view as well.

When I pulled up to the arena, however, things weren't exactly perfect. Signs for a motocross event—acrobatic racing on motorcycles—were plastered all over the place. The arena's owners had trucked in tons of dirt, and had bulldozed it into hills and moguls for motocross.

There was even less room for my round pen than there had been back in the church. In fact, there wasn't a flat piece of ground to be found anywhere on the floor of that arena.

"Don't worry," my friend from the church said. "The owners promised to bulldoze everything flat by Sunday morning."

As you can probably guess, when we arrived on Sunday morning, there was still hardly a flat piece of ground in that arena. In desperation, I jerry-rigged my round-pen panels into a rectangular pen between two of the hills. That proved to be less than ideal, and though we soldiered on, I could tell the crowd was disappointed.

I need to do something to catch their attention, I thought. *And I've got just the thing for it.*

Slipping out the gate of the pen, Spark and I rode right up the stairs of the bleachers, and into the second level, where we rode from side to side. Bleachers are not exactly a horse's idea of a great place to ride. They don't like the echoes of their hooves on the metal surfaces, or being that close to a crowd of people. And they certainly don't like to walk up and down stairs.

But nothing fazes Spark these days. The last time he was startled by anything came when we rode through the ballroom at the Hilton Hotel and Convention Center in New Orleans. As we rode up on stage, a camera focused on Spark and projected his image on the big screen in the convention center. Spark was startled for a minute, seeing himself on a big screen. Then he turned and walked nonchalantly away.

As we rode through the arena and down from the bleachers, a cheer rose up from the crowd. *That'll give them something to remember,* I thought, as Spark and I rode into the sunset.

Chapter 9

Overcoming Past Failures

THIS PAST CHRISTMAS I went to jail to see my son.

It wasn't exactly the kind of holiday experience that gets pictured on a Hallmark greeting card. There were no festive lights and laughter, no happy family gathered around the Christmas tree, opening presents and singing carols. But that's the way life is for our family right now.

Not long ago, Jeremiah was sentenced to nine years in prison, and is currently serving his time at the Coxsackie Correction Facility in Coxsackie, New York. Since he could not come home for Christmas—obviously—Melodie and I, along with our other son, Daniel, went to see him.

Again, it wasn't a Hallmark moment. But we were glad for the chance to be together. Daniel, who was just back from a tour of duty in Iraq, hadn't seen his brother for several years, and they had a bittersweet reunion—glad to see each other, but saddened by the circumstances that led to Jeremiah being in jail. It's not the way life is supposed to turn out. But then again, it's the way life is for the Sterretts.

Like any couple who have been married for more than a few years, our lives haven't been perfect. While most people are able to keep their difficulties behind closed doors—keeping their skeletons in the closet—that's not been our experience.

When your child goes to jail, you have two choices. You can cut off contact completely and erase any trace of them from your life. Or you can choose to love your child, no matter what.

The first choice is understandable. We've shed a lot of tears over the years for Jeremiah and watched him go through a great deal of heartache. I'm on the road most of the time these days, speaking at churches and conferences, and I often speak to married couples or groups of fathers and sons. Sometimes I wonder what I'm doing—if my own family isn't perfect, what right do I have to stand up and speak?

There have been times when I wanted to withdraw, shut down, and never speak to a group again. And there have been many times when I have wished my life was different.

But God hasn't allowed me to wallow in that kind of self-pity, no matter how tempting that is. Instead, every time I've wanted to quit, God's given me just enough prompting and spurring to keep going.

I mentioned earlier that couples often come to see

Melodie and me when they are at their wits' end; when every other attempt to save their marriage has failed. Sometimes I think we should hang a sign up that says, "If you are desperate, we can help."

Not that we are experts at marriage. Sometimes when we speak, people introduce us as relationships experts, as if we've discovered some hidden secret about marriage, and if a couple will only follow our advice, they'll live happily ever after and never have a problem again.

By now you've guessed that's not true. But what we have learned is how to pick up the pieces of life that fall apart. We bring hope to people because we have been through difficult times and have come through them stronger. I don't want people to learn how to survive those hard times. I want them to find enough hope that they can thrive as a result of those hard times. If we had not struggled, we'd have no hope to offer people.

That's what brought us to prison this past Christmas. We're hoping for a miracle, that Jeremiah's life can be healed. But miracles and redemption don't come when we sit around waiting for them. They come when we get up and begin taking small steps toward redemption.

There's a story told in the New Testament about the time that Jesus fed 5,000 people, who'd come out to the wilderness to hear him speak. The story is a familiar one but there's one aspect that always strikes me.

At one point in the story, the disciples come to Jesus and ask him to send the crowds away. After all, it's getting late and people are hungry. The disciples want Jesus to call a dinner break, and send the crowds to forage for food on their own. Instead, Jesus tells the disciples to serve a meal to the crowd.

Feeding a group of 5,000 people is a major undertaking. At the ranch, if we were preparing a meal for that many people, it'd take weeks of planning ahead, of ordering extra food, and putting up tents and renting extra kitchen equipment, and bringing in added help to get the meal prepared. It's not like whipping up a meal for a few dinner guests.

While the disciples wander around, complaining about how unfair Jesus is being to them, and how he's asked them to do the impossible, a little boy steps forward. In his hand are five loaves and two fish, and he offers them to Jesus.

That one small act opens up the space for Jesus to do something remarkable. By the time the meal is over, all 5,000 people have been fed, and there are twelve baskets full of fish and bread left over.

I've never seen 5,000 people fed with five loaves and two fish. What I have seen, though, are remarkable turnarounds that started with very small steps, like the ones taken by that little boy, almost 2,000 years ago.

Just before he died, Mike Yaconelli gave an interview, where he talked about the power of what he called small acts of grace. Yaconelli had written a book called *Messy*

Spirituality, where he talked about the struggles that most people, even those with deep faith, face. And he talked about the way that our modern secular society can squash the faith out of people.

"Our secular pagan culture doesn't make us get drunk, it makes us dull," he said. "It robs us of our creativity. We don't sit around thinking, how can I redeem this situation? We have lost the power of the tiny, of the small, of the little thoughtful things that we can do for each other that will make all the difference in the world. That's what happens in a pagan culture. It's not that we run around doing these horrible sins. It's that we don't run around doing these little acts of grace that we ought to be doing."

Of course, none of this means that life will turn around in an instant. In some ways, repairing or redeeming the life of a horse or a human being is harder than feeding 5,000 people. Often it takes thousands of tiny steps of faith and years of setbacks and stumbling, when you are tempted to throw in the towel, before a single life can be turned around.

Jeremiah has made major progress towards healing, towards putting his life back together. If we shunned him, that journey would be a great deal longer and a great deal more difficult.

No matter what, we won't do that. Not because we are great parents, but because Jeremiah and his brother Daniel have taught us the power of unconditional love.

Learning to love the boys wasn't easy. Not because of anything they had done, but because of how Melodie and I met them. Like most newlywed couples, we'd started out with dreams for having children and starting a family. Within a few years, it became clear that something was wrong. No matter how hard we tried, Melodie wasn't getting pregnant.

We eventually visited several doctors, who told us that we were infertile. A surprising number of people have trouble getting pregnant, and for them infertility is an emotional roller coaster. Each month begins with hope and ends with sorrow.

The Bible often refers to couples who don't have children as being barren, and the word fits. These days, doctors prefer the term "infertility," but that word lacks the punch and emotional heartache conveyed in the word "barren."

Because we were in ministry and had literally thousands of people coming through the ranch, word of our circumstances got around. Several people came forward, wondering if we'd be open to adopting a child. They knew of young women facing an unplanned pregnancy, who weren't able to care for a baby and wanted to place their child in a good home.

During those years, on several occasions we had opportunities offered to us, to adopt infants. So we did what all expecting parents do. We bought baby clothes and furniture, painted the nursery, and made space in our home for this new life.

At the last minute, these offers fell through. The first

time that happened, it was like a body blow, with all of our hopes being dashed. But we still held on to hope that the next time would be different. By the last time, we were wrung out emotionally, and wondered what we'd done to deserve this pain. Those were not easy years.

In our outreach to children, we worked with several foster agencies. Through that process we met Daniel and Jeremiah and felt clearly led to adopt them. They were half brothers, with the same mom but different dads, and both had had traumatic upbringings. I won't go into all the details—that's their story to tell, not mine.

As a result of their early struggles, life was hard for Daniel and Jeremiah. They had a lot of damage to undo. It took us years to realize how much they'd suffered before we knew them.

When you become a parent, it's a life long commitment. Before Daniel and Jeremiah came on the scene, I thought I knew what love was. I was wrong.

Over the last twenty years those boys have broken my heart. They have filled my life with joy. They stretched me beyond my limits many times. And they taught me that love is a choice. I love my sons, not because of their accomplishments, but because they are my sons.

Several years ago, I wrote them both a letter. For years, I realized, I'd projected my expectations on them. Most of those expectations were good—I want my boys to be honest, caring, strong men of character. Others weren't so good.

In some ways I wanted them to succeed in order to validate my status as their father. When they failed, though I never said it out loud, they could sense my disappointment, like a weight hanging over them.

Knowing that, I wrote them each a letter, telling them that I loved them, and releasing them from having to live up to my expectations. I blessed them, and told them that no matter what, I would always be grateful to be their father. They taught me how to love, and how to be a father, and I wanted them to know I was thankful.

Those letters, and our subsequent conversations, have changed our relationship. They don't have to worry about disappointing me any more. I still have hopes and dreams for them, but I want them to know that they are loved simply for who they are, and not for their accomplishments.

The inspiration for that letter came from an unlikely source—my stepfather. For years we'd been estranged, and I'd lost touch with him after he and my mother divorced. I hated him when I was younger, and went out of my way to point that out whenever I could. I'd ignore my stepfather, or disrespect him, or even provoke him as a teenager, refusing to give him any respect. He was not my father and I went out of my way to make that point any time I had the chance. In time I learned how to push his buttons, adding tension to our already stress-filled home. He and my mother had a rocky relationship already, and my behavior only made matters worse.

By the time I'd reached my twenties, regret began to sink in over the way I'd treated my stepdad. I like to say that God got a hold of me, and pointed out that I'd been a jerk. One of the Ten Commandments is to honor your mother and father, and I'd broken that one on a number of occasions.

Whatever my stepfather's shortcomings, he didn't deserve the kind of treatment I gave him. I didn't even show him the kind of common courtesy I showed to strangers. In short, I'd been a jerk. In my twenties, I began to realize that I had a lot to apologize for.

After tracking down my stepfather's address, I wrote out a letter, telling him how sorry I was for the way I'd acted, and how much I regretted it. Sometimes you write a letter like that, and then lose the courage to send it. Instead it ends up in the trash or in a drawer somewhere.

I was so convicted about my actions, and so desperate to take responsibility for them, that I dropped it in the mailbox, with more than a little bit of fear and trembling. Then I waited for a response. It never came, so I summoned up the courage to call him.

To my surprise, he was glad to hear from me. He accepted my apology, and said he'd regretted the distance that had come between us. He wished that we had been closer when I was growing up and that things could have been different between us.

That wasn't all he said. "I forgive you," he told me. "And I give you my blessing."

He had every right to withhold that forgiveness. My mother and he had long been divorced, and he didn't owe me anything. I don't even know if we were technically related anymore. None of that seemed to matter to my stepdad.

His words released me from the guilt and regret I'd carried for years. Now I wanted to pass that same kind of grace on to my sons.

The writer of the Old Testament book Isaiah knew something about that kind of grace as well. The prophet was speaking to people who were exiled—at this time, the Babylonians had conquered Israel, and driven the people far from their homes. Some were slaves, and some were refugees, with little hope that life could ever get better. Isaiah wrote:

> The Spirit of the Lord GOD is upon me, because the LORD hath anointed me to preach good tidings unto the meek; he hath sent me to bind up the brokenhearted, to proclaim liberty to the captives, and the opening of the prison to them that are bound; To proclaim the acceptable year of the LORD, and the day of vengeance of our God; to comfort all that mourn; To appoint unto them that mourn in Zion, to give unto them beauty for ashes, the oil of joy for mourning, the garment of praise for the spirit of heaviness; that they might be called trees

of righteousness, the planting of the LORD, that he might be glorified.

(*ISAIAH 61:1–3*)

That phrase, "beauty for ashes" has always struck me. Most of the things that matter in my life began as ashes and were turned into something beautiful. The ranch, my family, my work with horses, even becoming a father, all began with heartache and struggle. Over the years, they've been transformed and rebuilt into something great.

It's a bit like the way pearls are made. They begin when a parasite or some other irritant invades the mouth of an oyster. That invader irritates the sensitive parts of the oyster, and in response, the oyster begins to cover the intruder with layers of minerals. In this process, the oyster creates a pearl of great price.

I should not have been surprised at the irony that my broken relationship with my stepfather Earl Berry, and the difficulty that I had to work through with my horse Berry, would prove to be irritants that would result in pearls of wisdom.

I got the first glimpse of what that phrase—ashes to beauty—meant almost forty years ago, when I first began working with horses.

Our neighbors, the Fultons, spent many weekends at

horse shows and competitions, and they often invited me to go along. They'd load up their horses in the back of a horse van, fill the cab with kids, and off we'd go.

One of the regulars at the local horse shows was a woman whose name I have forgotten, who rode a dark bay gelding named Tweedy. Without fail, the two of them were among the best teams in the local shows. They rode in perfect unison, and seem to win while hardly breaking a sweat. There was something effortless about their performances.

At the time, I assumed that Tweedy was a ringer. This lady only had one horse, and didn't have a reputation as a great trainer, so I assumed she'd gone out and bought an expensive, fancy, well-trained horse, and that's why he rode so well.

It was then that I learned the truth. Tweedy wasn't a fancy horse at all. In fact, this woman had bought him at a horse auction, where his former owners were dumping him for pennies on the dollar. Tweedy was hardly more than skin and bones when she brought him home, and he'd been malnourished and neglected for some time.

Tweedy had hit rock bottom and been thrown on the trash heap. That's where his rider had found him. I don't know why she bought him—whether it was out of pity or compassion or if he was the only horse she could afford. But much like the great thoroughbred Seabiscuit, who'd been lingering in low-level claiming races before being rescued by his trainer, Tom Smith, there was more to Tweedy than met the eye.

His new owner put Tweedy on a healthy diet, fattened him up, and began to rebuild him with care and love and lots of exercise. Then she trained him.

Here's what struck me about Tweedy: He didn't just survive under her care, he blossomed. He gained confidence and always seemed eager to please. Together, they had a great partnership for many years.

The horse world can be a bit funny. We think that a horse is in its prime when it is young, between the ages of two and seven—that's when they are the strongest, fastest, and the most capable. But they spend relatively few years in that prime of life.

If a horse is in good shape when they are seven, they'll likely be active for another fifteen to twenty years. The quality of those years is based on how their training went in the early years. If they have a good foundation, they'll become a great horse for kids or grandkids, or amateur riders. Their best years become the decades they spend training young riders.

When I start training a horse, I'm not only thinking about the task at hand, or even what I'm going to teach six months down the road; I want the horse to learn the habits that will last for a lifetime, and then to be able to pass them on.

We call that mentoring, and I often use Spark to demonstrate how it works. It's not always easy. Spark's a stallion, and if you've spent any time around stallions, you'll know that they are territorial by nature. More than anything, they are really big boys who don't like to share. In the wild, and often in captivity, stallions will mark their territory and defend it fiercely from any horse who infringes on their space.

If there is a mare around, then as the saying goes, boys will be boys. Think of a stallion as a teenaged boy on steroids, and you'll get the idea.

When I train a stallion like Spark or Spotlight or my youngest horse, Romeo, I want them to set aside their aggression, their territoriality, and even their hormones, and focus all of their attention on me. That may sound selfish on my part, but it's not. In the end, I have their best interests at heart.

As long as a stallion is ruled by his emotions, he'll never reach his full potential, or be able to think clearly in a crisis, or when another horse is losing its mind. Once they have control of their emotions and can look to me—that's a different story.

Of course, even I have trouble reining in my emotions sometimes. Like the time I was flying through the air and about to land in an audience member's lap.

Spark and I were training an unbroken gelding, and things were not going quite as I planned. Most times when I pony another horse to Spark, by dallying their lead rope to my saddle horn, things go well. The untrained horse will mimic Spark's actions, shortening the training process as it learns by doing.

When things don't go well, that's when I have come to rely on Spark. With this gelding, things were not going well. I've had unbroken horses kick out at Spark or try and bite him, but that is par for the course. In fact, I usually put special pads on his legs to protect him from any kind of permanent injury.

We were in Washington State, doing a Sermon on the Mount presentation, when this gelding did something I'd not thought possible. We were by the edge of the arena, and suddenly he lurched towards Spark, throwing all of his weight against him, and knocking my stallion clear off his feet. I went flying over the fence and into the lap of a startled audience member.

Luckily I kept my head and didn't express my true feelings into the wireless microphone I wore. "Well, folks," I said, "things don't always go this well."

Then I jumped over the fence and got back at it. Spark had regained his feet by this time, and glanced at the gelding with a wary eye. But it takes more than that to deter Spark and myself. In a few minutes, we were leading the gelding back in the arena, with a little less slack on the lead rope so he couldn't pick up steam. Once he realized that we weren't impressed by his antics, the gelding calmed down and got with the program.

A similar thing happened in North Carolina, where I was working with a Trakehner mare, who'd never been ridden.

Trakehners are European warmblood horses, bred for their strength and athleticism, and are one of the larger breeds of horses. They're called warmbloods because they are descended from both "hot-blooded horses," like Arabians, who are known for their speed and high-strung personalities, and "cold-blooded horses," like draft horses, who are usually strong and steady.

This mare, who was heavily muscled, was at least a foot taller than Spark and outweighed him by several hundred pounds. She had no interest in cooperating with us, and resented being led by a smaller and lighter horse. So the mare launched a mini protest, right in the middle of the arena.

Without warning, she threw herself on the ground, laid out flat, and refused to move. If you're a parent, this may sound familiar, as two-year-olds often try this technique. It's meant to wear down a parent's or authority figure's patience. The idea is to become such a pain that the parent will give up, thinking that fighting with the child is not worth the effort.

I've been at this too long to fall for a trick like that, so I gently flicked a rope across her nose and the mare popped back to her feet. It was just enough to let her know that I wasn't impressed.

A few other things are worth noting. When I pony another horse, Spark is usually without a bridle. That's to make a point. When Spark is bridleless, he's under no compulsion to follow my lead. He follows my instructions because he wants to, not because he has to. Also, I don't have to worry about the other horse getting tangled in my reins.

On the other hand, at times the untrained horse won't do what they are told, even though I've got a lead rope tied to them. No matter what the other horse does, Spark ignores their bad behavior. He also controls his own hormones. Like I said, Stallions are like teenaged boys on steroids, and they usually find a mare irresistible. I've seen mares literally throw themselves at Spark, and he won't respond to their advances.

This particular mare, however, had no interest in anyone but herself. Within a few minutes of getting back on her feet, she tried the flopping act again. This second time, she refused to get up, even after I flicked her with a rope.

Undaunted, I hopped off and took a hold of her nose, and gave it a gentle squeeze. Not enough to hurt but enough to get her attention, because it cut off a little of her breathe. Once again, she hopped to her feet. The audience was impressed by the response, and by Spark's steadfastness, despite her antics.

One of the keys to our success in the Sermon on the Mount is that, for the most part, we've lost any fear of being embarrassed, and so we aren't ashamed to fail. I've got a saying: Anything worth doing, is worth doing poorly.

It's not that I don't believe that excellence matters. Quite the opposite. The only way to do something with excellence is to start out doing things poorly, and then learn from your mistakes.

A number of years ago, the owners of the Singing Pines Plantation in Glenwood, Georgia, asked to me to come down and work with some of their young colts. We were doing a round pen session, and they brought in a three-year-old for me to work with. He was a beautiful sorrel colt with a chiseled face, a powerful physique, and a mahogany red coat. The owners were planning on selling him, and thought his session with me might attract a buyer.

That first session didn't go very well. This particular colt had been left on his own most of the time, and so he wasn't domesticated enough for me to get close to him. He had a long reach with his front feet and had become quite accomplished at striking out with them. Every horse has its preferred method of defense. Some buck, some bite, some kick out with their hind legs, while others strike out with their front.

I'd not worked with this bloodline of Quarter Horse much before, and this colt was giving me a crash course. At first, his owners were miffed—they thought I was making their horse look bad. His aggressive behavior reflected poorly on them, and made a poor advertisement for this colt.

But as I worked the colt, I began to understand what made him tick. We got him settled down, and I put the lessons I learned with him to use with the next colt I worked with. Things went so well after that, that they'd invite me down every year to break in that year's group of colts.

It would have been easy to give up after the first day at the Singing Pines. I've got no interest in being kicked by a horse, or in upsetting the good people who'd invited me into their ranch.

By seeing it as a learning experience, and by not being afraid to fail, that first day at Singing Pines became the basis for a long-time friendship. Eventually the owners would give me Spotlight.

There's a bit of ironic twist to the story. Spotlight is a Quarter Horse, and on the day he was born, the president of one of the Quarter Horse clubs happened to be visiting Singing Pines. Even on that first day, Spotlight was a stunning colt, with a perfect physique and a golden coat, that made him seem a perfect specimen. The club president was so taken with Spotlight that he offered to buy him right then and there.

"He's not for sale," the owners said, but the president insisted. He pulled out his checkbook, tore off a check, signed it, handed the blank check to the owners of Singing Pines, and said, "You fill in the amount."

As he said that, Spotlight turned around, and the president's jaw dropped. On one side, Spotlight had a perfect golden coat. On the other side, however, he had a large white spot—as if someone had turned a spotlight on him. At the time, that discoloration made him worthless. He was disqualified from being registered as a Quarter Horse, and while he could be registered as a Paint Horse, he would be an unlikely Paint Stallion, because of his Quarter Horse bloodlines.

My friends who owned the Singing Pines handed the check back to the horse club president with a knowing smile. They were disappointed as well, knowing that this colt who they'd had such high hopes for had an uncertain future.

Things turned out all right in the end. Spotlight came to Miracle Mountain Ranch and began his training. Meanwhile, my friends at the Singing Pines suggested I should not give up hope for Spotlight's future. The Quarter Horse Association was considering changing its rules to allow Paint Horses to be cross-registered as Quarter Horses. When that happened this once worthless horse became a rarity—a Quarter Horse and a Paint Stallion, and worth far more than the average Quarter Horse.

There is one other reason that I've learned to never give up hope. That's because I've lived long enough to know that in life, anything can happen. Just ask my friend Ralph.

For more than thirty years, Ralph has been my right-hand man at the ranch. He runs the summer camp, works with our apprentices, and specializes in working with difficult campers—those who don't think the rules apply to them. Ralph's an expert with those kinds of kids, because he used to be one.

Ralph first came to Miracle Mountain Ranch more than

forty years ago, as an eight- or nine-year-old boy. By that time, he'd already been thrown out of three other camps, and—after arriving at the ranch—tried to make it four.

If not for Dale Linebaugh, Ralph might have succeeded. But Dale had a way with boys like Ralph, and as Ralph's mother drove off, Dale put his firm but gentle hand on the back of his neck, gave a squeeze, and said, "We're going to get along just fine." And they did, though Ralph gave Dale a run for his money. (Little did Ralph know that he'd spend most of the rest of his life at the ranch.)

Years later, Ralph repaid Dale's investment as he sat with an eight-year-old named Jeremiah Beize at the dining-room table while the other campers had gone, insisting that Jeremiah could leave as soon as he finished his dinner.

No matter how Jeremiah fumed or screamed, "Help, they are killing me!", Ralph sat without reacting, as if he had all the time in the world. Ralph knew that on the inside, Jeremiah wasn't a bad kid. But he was angry at his abusive parents and the foster-care system. One year later, Jeremiah would become Dale's grandson and our son.

Ralph's parents' divorce had driven a wedge between Ralph and his mom as well. Though she cared for him, and made sure he always had enough to eat and had clothes on his back, she withheld any words of love or appreciation.

By the time he'd arrived at the ranch, Ralph had also been suspended several times from school for fighting. He and his mom moved often when he was growing up, and he was often a target for bullies as the new kid in town.

But Ralph was strong and tough for his size. So whenever he moved to a new school, he figured out who the biggest bully was, and picked a fight with that kid. Most of the time Ralph won the fights, ensuring that other bullies would leave him alone. If there was going to be a fight, Ralph made sure he got the first punch in.

Ralph came to the ranch with that chip on his shoulder, daring the other campers or anyone in authority to knock it off. But Dale knew that Ralph's attitude was mostly an act. Once you got past that outer shell, there was a boy who missed his father and didn't know what to do with that anger. His gentle but firm response eventually defused Ralph's anger, and began to turn his life around. When I became the ranch's director, Ralph was one of the first people I hired.

Despite all his success at the camp, there was one thing still missing from his life. It could be summed up in three simple words that Ralph's mother had never spoken to him in his nearly fifty years of life. Just three simple words: "I love you."

Every time he talked to his mother, Ralph made a point of telling her that he loved her. At first she ignored him. Then, when they were talking on the phone, she'd pause after saying goodbye, waiting for him to say, "I love you."

After two years, she was finally able to say, "Um hum,"

after he told her that he loved her. But still, she couldn't say the words.

Finally, after three years, she ended a phone call by saying, "I love you."

Some things are worth waiting for, even if it takes fifty years.

Chapter 10

A Responsible Choice

WHEN I WAS SEVENTEEN, God snuck up on me.

My family was Presbyterian, and when it came to going to church, my mother didn't mess around. She often spent her night reading the Bible into the wee hours of the morning, and she made sure we were found every Sunday sitting in the pews of our home church, until I was teenager.

When I joined 4-H, however, my mother began to ease up. Many of the horse shows and other 4-H events were scheduled on Sundays, and reluctantly, she let me skip out on services.

After a couple of years, I became an expert on getting out of church. If it wasn't a 4-H event, then I'd say that I had some chores to do at the neighbors' farms, or some work to do on my horses. I always had some kind of excuse handy.

My mother wasn't pleased, but as long as I promised to read my Bible to make up for missing church, she'd give in. This infuriated my stepfather, but my mother would always cover for me. Things were already tense enough at home, and she wanted to avoid making church one more battleground. She was working diligently to hang on to me.

In 1970, I won the statewide veterinary science and horse project competitions for 4-H, which meant a trip to Chicago, Illinois, for the national conference. That year marked the fiftieth anniversary of 4-H, and among the celebrities making an appearance at the event was then-President Richard Nixon. The Ford Motor Company was one of the main sponsors, and the convention promised to be quite a show.

I was glad to be away from home, and was looking forward to having a good time, far away from my mother's watchful eye. I wasn't a bad kid or a troublemaker back then, but I'd started rebelling against my mother's strict rules about drinking and smoking, or spending too much time hanging out with girls.

We arrived at the hotel in downtown Chicago on Saturday, and had Sunday morning free. Some of the kids I was hanging out with wanted to go over to the Moody Bible Church, a Chicago institution founded by the famed evangelist Dwight L. Moody. I thought, *Oh, stink! Not church!*

Then again, there was this pretty girl in the group. She was Miss Rodeo Washington State, and I thought, *I'd like to have some of her attention.* When we talked, she mentioned that she was going to church the next morning, and hoped I was going too. Since she was going to church, I was willing to go.

As far as Miss Rodeo Washington State went, church was a lousy investment—she soon lost interest in me. I even tried writing to her once the convention was over, but after an initial response, she eventually stopped replying. I should have slept in or gone down to the pool instead.

Still, that Sunday's service wasn't a complete waste of time. I'd heard lots of sermons growing up, and most had gone in one ear and out the other. For some reason, the sermon in that Chicago service got through. The preacher's name has escaped me, but the Bible passage he used that morning still echoes in my mind. It was from the Gospel of Matthew, where Jesus talked about what really matters in life. Jesus said:

> If anyone would come after me, he must deny himself
> and take up his cross and follow me. For whoever
> wants to save his life will lose it, but whoever loses
> his life for me will find it. What good will it be for a
> man if he gains the whole world, yet forfeits his soul?
> Or what can a man give in exchange for his soul?
>
> (MATTHEW 16:24–26 NIV)

That question lingered in my mind as I made my way back to the hotel. What good is it to gain the whole world—money, success, fame—if it costs you your soul?

Winning a 4-H national championship is not the kind of thing that people sell their soul for. I'd won three of those, and had started to see that winning didn't make me feel any better about myself, at least not in the long run.

The desire to win was making me push my horses harder and harder, without much concern beyond the next trophy. While it worked in the short run, even then I knew I was on shaky ground. The harder I pushed them, the more likely one of the horses was going to crack, and not be able to handle the pressure. In the back of my mind, I knew that pushing them so hard wasn't good for them in the long run.

There were also temptations in the horse show world. There was a lot of money at stake for a trainer who could consistently produce winners. That money added to the pressure to succeed in the show ring. Even then, I knew that money alone wasn't going to make me happy.

Though I wouldn't have admitted it at the time, I didn't like the person I was becoming. I had the reputation for being a straight-laced kid, and so I played that up in public. When I was with my friends, I'd swear and drink and chase girls, but when I was at shows or 4-H events, I put on the face of a good Christian boy.

That act got me in good with a girl named Cindy Biel. She was sixteen, and her dad was a prominent horse dealer in a neighboring county. He sold horses and tack, and all the other paraphernalia from the horse show world.

Cindy was a sweet girl, and she was into 4-H, so we ended up spending a lot of time together. Later on, she invited me to spend time with her family, and I hit it off with them as well. I began to think that this was the kind of family I'd really like to be a part of.

Almost ten years after his death, the loss of my father still felt like a heavy weight on my chest. So much had changed since then. We'd lost the farm, our family had splintered, and the grief over an absent dad was always there in the background.

Much like a horse who'd been separated from the herd and run in off the range, I felt corralled, wishing there was some way I could hop the fence and find some release from my painful loneliness.

Cindy's dad, Mr. Biel, was the kind of father figure I craved. If I could find another family to be a part of, I told myself that I could be happy. I liked Cindy, and I liked her family, and I thought if things worked, this is the kind of family I'd always wanted to be a part of. I was still a kid then, so I wasn't thinking seriously about marriage, but the thought of a future with Cindy and her family crossed my mind more than a few times.

My wife, Melodie, sometimes kids me that I married her for her dad, and she's more than a little bit right. In Mr. Biel, I saw some of the same characteristics that would later draw me to Dale Linebaugh.

One night, some of my friends and I decided to hang out at the sale barn. The barn was filled with teens and adults, hanging out while the sale went on in the background.

While I was walking around the outside, suddenly,

someone came up from behind and grabbed me. They put their hands over my eyes, so I couldn't see who it was. I figured it was one of my friends, playing a trick on me, so in order to impress my friends, I responded in a coarse and arrogant manner.

Then I heard the deep voice of Mr. Biel ring in my ears. "Well, if that's the way you feel about it," he said. He let go of me, and walked off into the dark. I could have slid under the lowest door-sill; I felt that embarrassed and that small. This man had seen right through me.

Mr. Biel taught me a valuable lesson that night. To really know someone, watch their reactions, not their actions. I realized that I am never the man of my actions—I'm always the man of my reactions. I've never forgotten that lesson.

That night I saw myself painfully clear, and the view wasn't pleasant. The vulgar words weren't the main problem. In essence, I'd become two-faced, putting on a good show when it was to my advantage, but hiding what I was really like on the inside.

I use that lesson often while training horses. On the surface, a horse can seem perfectly well mannered and trustworthy. But you never know what a horse is capable of until you push them out of their comfort zone.

Some of the owners who come to me, asking for help with their horses, have been riding time bombs, and they never knew it. Push a horse a bit too far and they'll react, showing their true personality.

Before I ever saddle a horse, I wrap a rope around his body, following the same pattern that the saddle girth will take. I want to see how the horse will respond when those girths are tightened.

I don't do it quickly—I prepare the horse by putting the rope over his head and laying a blanket on his back, and rewarding him for remaining calm. I use the rope to make sure he is ready. The last thing I want is to be on a horse's back and have him lower the hammer on me.

That's exactly what happened to a friend of mine. She'd been training dressage horses for years, and finally had acquired the horse of her dreams. Dressage is sometimes called a ballet for horses, where athleticism and agility are highly prized.

My friend had found the perfect horse for the event from a breeder in Holland. The horse was a Hanoverian, the perfect combination of agility and strength for dressage. Even before the horse arrived at her farm, she imagined them becoming champions.

Because he was a costly investment, my friend had a thirty-day grace period before the final payment was due. That first month was like being on a honeymoon. The horse was everything my friend had hoped for. Not only was he talented and capable as a performer, but he was also responsive and enthusiastic as a training partner. He did what she asked him to do, without a moment's hesitation or complaining.

But as most of us know, the honeymoon has to end someday. No sooner had my friend signed the contract and sent the final payment, than this new horse showed his true colors.

My friend went out to work with her horse, as she'd done for a month, and he turned on her. As she climbed in the saddle, he bolted and sent her flying. She ended up lying flat on her face in the dirt, while her dream horse ambled off, as if nothing was out of the ordinary.

By the time she called me, my friend had been dumped five or six times, and was in a panic. The horse had cost her tens of thousands of dollars, and now she wondered if she'd flushed that money down the toilet and was left with a worthless horse.

I wasn't quite as bad as that Hanoverian. But I'm not sure any one could really trust me. Push me too far, and there was no telling what I might do.

When I got to Penn State, there were more tests. On the outside, I was still Mr. Clean Cut. On the inside—well, that was another story.

Here was my problem in a nutshell: I couldn't change myself.

We see the same problem in a horse. A wild horse, or a horse who has grown up on a ranch or farm can't train itself. To reach his full potential, every horse needs to learn how to partner with his trainer or owner, and how to follow his direction. The horse needs someone to show the way.

My stepfather did that for me, when I wrote to him, asking for forgiveness. There was nothing I could do to make our relationship right. I could tell him I was sorry, and ask for forgiveness, but I could not make things right between us. Only my stepfather could do that. Once he forgave me, then relationship was restored.

It was the same, later on, with the staff at Miracle Mountain Ranch. They'd been hurt and felt taken advantage off, so they reacted in fear and mistrust when I took over the ranch. I could reach out my hand in friendship and ask them to follow, but I could not compel them to do it.

They had to take, in essence, a leap of faith, and put their trust in me. Or they could leave, and go someplace that better suited them. Unless they could set aside those hurts and trust me, they'd never be happy at the ranch.

At Penn State, I found a mentor in my friend and teacher, Ward Studebaker. Not only did he teach me about horses and character, but he taught me about God.

Like I said, I'd heard many sermons, but very few had ever gotten through to me. Ward did, however, in a very low-key and simple way.

When we were done with classes, I'd often talk with Ward about some of my struggles with drinking or other temptations on campus. He'd never tell me what to do. Instead, he'd say something like this: "I don't know, Lew, but the Bible says…" I don't even recall what verses in the Bible he pointed out. The thing that convicted me was that he had a foundation to stand on. When he needed to make a decision, he had a reliable source of wisdom to draw on, outside of his own feelings. Somehow the Bible and God were real to him.

That intrigued me. I thought, *I have no lighthouse, no guidepost, no standard to live by.* I didn't have the kind of confidence that Ward had.

Still, I wasn't much interested in God, no matter how much he was trying to get my attention. I wanted to enjoy my life, to have a good time, and I didn't want any God spoiling my plans. When I was old, then I'd have time for God.

I was really like a mustang, who'd been perfectly happy living out in the desert plains, and who now had been run into a corral and had to deal with a trainer who wanted to mess with his life.

There's a misperception about God in our culture, one that I used to fully embrace. God, so the conventional wisdom goes, wants to ruin your life. To know or follow God, I thought, meant giving up all of life's pleasures and becoming a shriveled prune of a puritan, afraid that someone, somewhere is having a good time. I thought being a Christian meant being miserable. I was mistaken.

More than anything, I was like that wild mustang, who'd rather stand by the edge of the round pen and look for a way to jump the fence and get back on the prairie, than turn to the trainer in the arena.

I came to understand that God didn't want to ruin my life. He wanted to offer me something better than wandering around the prairie on my own for the rest of my life. He wanted to give me a family and friends and a chance to do great things.

More than that, he wanted to forgive me, and help me take off the mask that I'd been wearing, and to take the burden of grief and anger from my father's death off my shoulders.

"Come to me, all you who are weary and burdened, and I will give you rest," Jesus once said. "Take my yoke upon you and learn from me, for I am gentle and humble in heart, and you will find rest for your souls. For my yoke is easy and my burden is light" (Matthew 11:28–30 NIV).

I had a need and I couldn't meet it, and so I needed help, just like a horse who can't do it on his own. I realized that Jesus came into my arena, like a trainer coming in to work with a horse, so that I would come to know and trust him. He didn't make me come to him, and require that I clean myself up and make myself worthy of his attention. He came into my life, as messy and unruly as it was, and embraced me just as I was. Just as I want a horse to take the initiative and move towards me, God wanted me to move towards him, and trust him.

In many ways I was like Spotlight, caught in the barbed wire on that Missouri mountainside. If I tried to wrench myself free, I'd only pull the wire tighter. I needed someone to come and cut the wire and show me the way to walk. And I needed to have enough trust in my Heavenly Trainer to overcome my natural inclination to run.

I needed help getting out of that snare. And help came in the form of Jesus, and of letting go of my past, and deciding to follow him.

It didn't all happen in an instant. God didn't ask me to take a leap of faith. Instead, he asked me to take one small step at a time. As those steps built one upon another, the course of my life began to change—acknowledging my desperate need, turning to the one God had sent, and asking God both to forgive me and to be the boss of my life.

The first step was found in chapter 10 of the New Testament book of Romans, which says that, "If you confess with your mouth, 'Jesus is Lord,' and believe in your heart that God raised him from the dead, you will be saved. For it is with your heart that you believe and are justified, and it is with your mouth that you confess and are saved" (verses 9–10 NIV).

That one small step of faith was the biggest step I would ever take, as it changed my life forever.

CHAPTER 11

FRUIT OF THE SPIRIT

EARLIER IN THIS BOOK, I made a confession: Though I've been a cowboy for nearly fifty years now, I still can't rope for beans.

If you've got a wild horse that's never been ridden, and you need someone to take him in a round pen and tame him, I'm your man. If you've got to have someone ride circles around breakfast tables in a hotel banquet hall on horseback, I've been there and done that.

Ask me to rope a horse—and things get ugly.

That's why I got up early one morning this past summer to take lessons from a teenager. We had a Sermon on the Mount presentation scheduled at the camp that day, and as part of that presentation, I planned to rope an untrained horse before ponying with Spark.

Roping is not my strong point at the best of times, so I decided a little practice was in order. That way I wouldn't completely embarrass myself in front of the crowd later on that evening.

With a target set up in the middle of the outdoor arena at the ranch, I got to work. Whirling the rope several times around my head, I took aim at the target, and let the rope fly.

Missed. The lasso sailed over the target, and landed in the sand.

Undaunted, I tried again. Whirl the rope, aim, toss the rope.

Missed. Deep breath. Whirl, aim, toss the rope.

Missed again. Another deep breath. Whirl, aim toss.

Got it!

This pattern went on for another hour. I was successful about 20 per cent of the time, or one out of every five throws, on a stationary target. It was going to be a long night.

About this time, Johnston Williams, one of our apprentices, happened by the arena. He'd grown up on a ranch, and had been roping cattle and horses from the time he could walk. He settled down on the fence to watch me practice, adding to my anxiety.

I was the supposed horsemanship expert, and he was spending two years as an apprentice at the ranch to learn from me and our staff. And now Johnston was going to see that I was struggling with a task he'd mastered as a kid. This was the last thing I needed. Or maybe it was just the thing I needed.

"Mind giving me some pointers here?" I asked, in a hopeful voice.

For more than thirty years, I've been preaching and practicing what's known as servant leadership. Rather than barking orders and expecting people to jump at my commands, I try to understand the needs of my staff first. Knowing their needs and personalities allows me to better serve them.

That doesn't mean that I'm always best buddies with my staff. The ranch isn't a democracy—I'm the boss. Still, I want my staff to be self-motivated, to see when something needs to be done, and do it, without waiting for instructions from me, and I also want them to function as a team.

It's the same way with my horses. I want them to be trustworthy and confident, to know how to react during a crisis, or when facing an obstacle.

Building confidence doesn't happen overnight. And it doesn't happen by me telling the staff, "Be confident," or holding motivational meetings. Confidence comes with practice.

I needed some pointers on roping. Johnston was the expert. The smart thing to do was to ask for his help. In my book, the leader always does the smart thing, rather than the thing that makes him look good.

For the next hour or so, I got a lesson in roping 101, and made subtle changes to my technique. By the end, I was hitting on four out of five throws—a vast improvement.

That night, my apprentice-turned-instructor sat on the fence and watched as I roped a wild horse on the first try.

Johnston smiled and raised his hands in a cheer, proud of my accomplishment and of his first success as a teacher.

I learned this approach to leadership the hard way. After graduating from Penn State, I spent a year in New York, studying at Nyack Bible College. Once I was done there, Melodie and I got married, and then started looking for the next step.

I had planned to go on to graduate school and work in the horse industry, but my new-found faith, and new marriage, got me thinking of more eternal values. Marrying Melodie did not make joining the family ministry a requirement, but it did open a wide door of opportunity.

For years, I'd built my identity around being a trainer, working with championship-caliber horses. As a result, I'd become a horse snob, thinking that only expensive horses were worth my time.

It wasn't that working with horses was wrong for me. But I had built my identity and my worth around the horse industry and what I could accomplish. I suddenly realized I was trusting more in that than what the Lord had for me. So I walked away from it. In the process, I got a lesson in humility.

In the summer of 1975, I got a call from the president of the Appaloosa Horse Club. They'd sponsored me when I was in college, and now the president wanted to offer me a job. I'd be his assistant, with the idea that he'd train me to succeed him when he retired.

This sounded like my dream job, and I was sorely tempted by the opportunity. In fact, I accepted the job just before Melodie and I got married, but didn't tell anyone about it, especially not her parents. There was no reason to ruin our wedding with the news. Dale and Opal hoped that we'd follow in their footsteps of serving the Lord, and taking this job would mean going in a different direction.

Around the same time, I heard about an opening at the Rawhide Vocational College in California. The school combined horse training with Christian ministry, so that young people would learn the horse business while growing in their faith. This job paled in comparison to the one I'd been offered at the Appaloosa Horse Club—a national breed association—so I put it out of my mind.

"I won't even talk to them unless someone else pays for the long-distance call," I told Melodie one day, as we were talking through our options for the future. That's the kind of thing you should never say. Later that night, we were visiting with Melodie's parents when a friend of the family stopped by. He'd heard about this job in California and thought it'd be a perfect place for me to start.

"Tell you what," he said. "Pick up the phone right now, and I'll even pay for the call."

Oh stink, I thought.

A few weeks later, we were on our way to California. It seemed clear that God wanted us to take this job. In fact, when I'd balked at the cost of flying out to California for the interview—this was a non profit camp—another family friend gave us $400 for the plane tickets.

After a few months on the job, I wondered what I'd got myself into. The pay was poor, and though the horses were above average, and some were even world champions, my boss—well, he was a tough man to follow. It's not that he was angry or abusive. Not at all. In fact, he treated Melodie and me well in the two years we spent there. But as a boss, he was a disaster.

The major problem was that he was impulsive by nature, so he was always changing his mind. One day he'd tell you to start working on a project and the next he'd tell you to abandon that and jump on something else. You never knew from one day to the next what he wanted.

He was also rough with the students, believing that shame was the best way to teach them. He had an uncanny ability to push people's buttons, to get them to do what he wanted, or to upset them.

When we arrived, less than a quarter of the students were making it through the two-year program, and staff turnover was even faster. Six months in, I was ready to quit.

Then a friend gave me some wise advice. "There's something you need to learn here," he said. My friend knew about my estranged relationship with my stepfather, and felt like that had left a flaw in my character. I'd never be a leader unless I learned how to be a follower.

Not exactly the advice I wanted to hear. Now, however, I realize he was right on. Like Berry, my horse with the congenital defect in his legs, I had a weakness in my character, and my new boss was like a personal trainer, attacking that character flaw. I needed to learn how to respect authority and how to be a follower.

When I work with an untrained horse, I can usually get them saddle-broken in around an hour and a half, even if they've been run in right off the plains. But that first step is only the beginning. It's a long, hard journey to turn that untrained horse into a trustworthy partner. When I start working a new horse, I know it'll be two or three years until my work pays off in his or her life.

Working at Rawhide, I learned that the same was true in my faith. The New Testament book of Galatians talks about the signs of a mature Christian, calling them the "fruits of the Spirit." Among those fruits are "love, joy, peace, patience, kindness, goodness, faithfulness, gentleness and self-control" (Galatians 5:22–23 NIV).

There's no magic pill you can take to make those character traits instantly appear in your life. You have to learn them over years of practice.

For those two years at Rawhide, I took a notebook with me everywhere I went, and began to write down my ideas about leadership. I wanted to know what motivated people, and discouraged them. In the end, I boiled them down to some simple truths.

Communicate clearly. That was the first and most important lesson. If people don't know what you want, they can't deliver it. This also means showing people how they fit into the bigger picture.

Prepare people for change, don't spring it on them. Over those two years, I learned that people don't mind following, if they believe their leader knows what he or she is doing. They also don't want to waste their time. There's nothing more disheartening than to spend days or weeks toiling on a project, only to find out you've been wasting your time. Before too long, people will slack off, believing that their hard work doesn't matter.

Correct people in private, not in public. Respect is perhaps the most important gift a leader can give. Respect your people, and let them use their talents. If they do something wrong, talk to them in private—don't embarrass them in front of their peers. Everyone wants to save face.

Deal with conflict immediately. If a problem arises, don't sweep it under the table. Deal with it head on, not with force, but with a listening ear. Chances are, if someone on your staff is angry or withdrawn, or upset at you, they've got a reason. Ask for their opinions, and then listen.

These lessons form the basis of my leadership style, with people and with horses.

Respect is a key factor here. When I work with a new horse, I never try to push them too far. I don't expect major leaps of faith. I want small, measurable steps toward success.

So whenever a horse does what I ask him to, I give him a reward, and back off the pressure. I respect that he has the ability to choose to do the right thing of his own volition.

The more you respect a horse, the more he will respect you as a person. When he respects you, and comes to believe that you have his best interests at heart, he'll take the initiative and move towards you.

When I try something new with a horse, I don't expect him to get it right the first time. More than anything, I want to know that he is listening and that he trusts me. When a horse looks at me and tells me, through his body language, that he is afraid or confused, but remains in place rather than following his natural inclination to flee—that means his whole value system has changed.

Those first few months in California, I was angry and disappointed, feeling that God was wasting my time. I had turned down the job of my dreams in order to follow what I thought was God's leading, and what had it gotten me? A miserable job.

Over the two years I worked at Rawhide, my attitude slowly changed. As I put those leadership principles into practice, the students responded. By the time we left, retention was up from less than 25 per cent to more than 90 per cent.

Many of those students remain friends to this day, and when we started Sermon on the Mount, they invited me to come and speak at their churches or camps. If I'd quit, none of those doors would have opened.

A few years after leaving Rawhide and going back to Miracle Mountain Ranch, I went to see the leader of another camp, looking for tips on how to become a better leader. It was a disappointment. He said I was too concerned about respecting the people who worked for me, which made me indecisive in his eyes.

"You'll never amount to much of a leader," he said. "You're too much of a nice guy." He was a bold, winner-take-all kind of leader, who always had to be in charge.

As much as his comments hurt, I didn't want to follow his example. I thought, *I will serve others and see what happens.*

Several years ago, Rich Stearns, a successful corporate CEO, decided to leave behind his corner office—and the Jaguar that came with it—to become director of World Vision, which is the largest Christian relief and development organization in the world. The idea was that Stearns' business acumen would help World Vision become more efficient at doing its job of feeding hungry people, providing clean water, caring for AIDS orphans and other acts of love in the name of Jesus.

During his first year on the job, Stearns didn't make any major changes. In fact, he didn't say much at all. Sometimes, when a business leader like Stearns comes to a nonprofit organization, they bring a chip on their shoulder, believing that the nonprofit world or ministry world is an easier place to work than the corporate world.

In an interview with *Christianity Today* magazine, Stearns said that business leaders often have a bias that goes something like this: "I know all the answers, because I played in the big leagues. This is the way it's going to be, and I'm going to change everything." That attitude is a recipe for failure, Stearns said.

"If I had come to World Vision saying, 'I know all the answers. Watch and learn,' World Vision would have rejected me as a leader like a body would reject a heart transplant as foreign tissue."

Instead, he took this approach: "I don't know the answers, but I think you do, and I want to learn from you. If you can teach me, and I can learn from you, then I hope to get to a place where I can add value to what you're doing."

In my early days of horse training, I spent much of my time at Colonial Acres, the farm owned by my boss, George Zimmerman. Most of the farm was on hillsides, spotted with outcroppings of limestone.

Among other things, that made it a pain to mow the grass that we'd bale to make hay. Being at Colonial Acres made me long to be back at the Fruitful Manor, which had been my family's farm before my dad died.

George eventually hired another trainer, who came from Texas, and he marveled at the hills on George's property. He insisted on exercising our colts on those hills. Before long, we had developed colts whose fitness and muscle tone made them winners.

The limestone in the soil also ensured that our grass was filled with minerals and other nutrients. Again, this new trainer pointed out that the rocky terrain was a benefit to our horses, not a detriment. I wasn't thinking about nutrition at that point—I was too busy complaining about how hard it was to mow those hills.

It was years before I realized that trainer was right. The broad green pastures, bordered by picket fences, look great on a postcard or in a painting hung on the wall. But we need the hills and obstacles in life to make us strong.

One reason that the horses at Colonial won so often, was that they were in better shape than the competition. The daily routine of running up those hills made them strong, and built up their endurance, so that they could train harder and longer than the average horse. More training and better endurance meant a better chance of winning.

Going to work for the Appaloosa Horse Club had been my dream. It's what I wanted. But what I needed and what I wanted were two different things. I needed to learn how to follow and persevere, even in difficult times.

There were times, however, when following what I thought was God's will was really difficult and even painful. I'd be lying if I said that I never wanted to quit. Chances are, if you're honest, most of us have felt that way at one point or another, whether it's in our marriage, or our work, or with our families.

One of the most popular hardcover books in U.S. history is called *The Purpose-Driven Life*. The idea of that book is relatively simple: God has a purpose for your life, and you'll never be truly satisfied until you find that purpose.

But what happens when you find your purpose in life, only to see all of your dreams go off the rails? When everything you hoped for has vanished in a puff of smoke— what do you do then?

I don't know what your life is like, or if you've ever felt like giving up. If it hasn't happened to you before now, praise the Lord. But it's going to happen someday. When that day comes, keep this story in mind.

In the early days of our leadership training seminars, when I was giving a talk about being a servant leader, a man in the front of the audience got up and boldly spoke out. He was a man in his seventies, and was visibly upset by something I'd said. I wasn't sure what to do, as nothing like this had ever happened before.

He stood up and pointed a finger at me and said, "Where

have you been all my life? Why didn't someone tell me this when I was younger, before it was too late?"

He sat down again and I froze for a moment. I had no idea how to respond. How do you answer a question like that? Though he had been faithfully religious all his life, he had suddenly realized the years spent living for himself had resulted in waste and disappointment.

Sometime later, this man called me, late at night, and asked if he and his wife could come in and see me. When they arrived at my office, I knew something was up. They both were irritable and visibly upset.

"We've been married fifty-three years," his wife said, "and I'm done with him."

Over the next few hours, they told me their story. After fifty-three years of marriage, they had quite a tale to tell. There'd been a great deal of betrayal; some of it was out in the open, some of it hidden for years.

"He's been lying to me from the beginning," she said. "Our whole marriage is a lie."

This wasn't quite true. After many years of marriage, there was plenty of blame to go around. Over those decades the fundamental trust that any relationship needs had been broken and crushed into the ground.

When couples come to see us, they are often desperate. In this case, the wife was so forlorn that at night, while her husband was asleep, she'd take out a gun and debate whether or not to shoot him and then end it all. After so many years of misery, this couple really were desperate.

Even in that darkest moment, there was the tiniest shred of hope. Like Spotlight stuck in the barbed wire, they were trapped. If they bolted and divorced, it would shatter their lives and the lives of their children and grandchildren. But they could not stay where they were either. They needed someone to show them the way out.

For Spotlight, that meant putting his fate in someone else's hands. In the end, that's what this couple did. Only they put their fate in the hands of God. Though they had long before heard and responded to the message of salvation, they had never really trusted in God's full control of their lives.

At their crisis point, they got on their knees and asked God for help. Rather than cling to their bitterness and hurt, they let go of their past, and chose to forgive each other.

In the prayer that Jesus taught his disciples, there's a line that fits here: "Forgive us our trespasses, as we forgive those who trespass against us." As they found God's forgiveness, they were able to forgive each other.

Over the next few months, they worked through the pain and disappointments, and began to trust each other once again. It was never easy and they wanted to give up. Like Spotlight, however, they eventually found their way out.

Today, this couple, and their children and grandchildren, are growing in their walks with God and in their marriages.

They sit together in church, filled with love and laughter, rather than the anger and despair that had defined their lives for so long. By any definition, that's a miracle worth believing in.

If God can save this couple when all hope was lost, he can save any hopeless situation. They discovered that true and lasting hope is found when absolute trust is placed in the person and work of Jesus Christ.

Join me on my journey of knowing the greatest trainer of all time—the Lord Jesus Christ.